ISMITH KHAN:

THE MAN & HIS WORK

ROYDON SALICK

ISMITH KHAN:

THE MAN & HIS WORK

PEEPAL TREE

First published in Great Britain in 2012
Peepal Tree Press Ltd
17 King's Avenue
Leeds LS6 1QS
England

ISBN13: 9781845231743

Supported using public funding by
ARTS COUNCIL
ENGLAND

CONTENTS

ACKNOWLEDGEMENTS

I would like to thank Farida and Jameen, Ismith's two children, Mariam Sherar and Vera Simone, Ismith's two former spouses, and Betty Nicolson, Ismith's companion of his last twenty-two years, and Zuleika and Rowena, Ismith's two sisters, for their interest in this project and their information in conversation and by email. Without the information they so readily provided, the biographical sketch would have been much less detailed, and dates would have been less trustworthy. I would also like to thank Mr Sookdeo Bhagwandeen of the library at The University of The West Indies, St Augustine, for his ever-willing assistance in sourcing critical material on Ismith Khan; he made this project much less difficult. A similar debt I owe to Roddy Batchasingh. I have found the bibliography of Neil Mohammed, a former graduate student of mine at UWI, St Augustine, who did a research paper on Ismith Khan, indispensable. Ken Ramchand has not only shared his thoughts about Ismith Khan and the West Indian novel, but also has been generous with his books and his encouragement. Moreover, Jeremy Poynting's judicious editing has improved the quality of the manuscript. Finally, my wife, Nalini, has helped tremendously with formatting the text.

For Brandon and Shannon

INTRODUCTION

I

Ismith Khan, known affectionately as "Sonny" to close friends and relatives, died in New York on April 21, 2002, one month after his seventy-seventh birthday, leaving two boxes of manuscripts and papers, and a corpus that comprises three novels and one collection of short stories. If we take at face value the publication dates of his first work, a short story entitled "In the Subway" (1955), and of his last work, *A Day in the Country & Other Stories* (1994), we assume that he had a writing career of almost four decades. The truth of the matter, however, is that most of Khan's writing was done between 1955 and 1972. Whatever writing he did in the 1970s and after amounted to revisions of his two unfinished, unpublished novels, "In Search of Stella" and "A Tale of Two Cities". Still, three novels and one collection of short stories make up a relatively small oeuvre, considering that in a similar period, Selvon had published seven novels and one collection of short stories. After *The Crucifixion*, written in 1970 and published in 1987, Khan changed the familiar Trinidadian setting that had served him so well in all his novels and short stories. He used New York as the setting of "In Search of Stella", and Mexico and California in "A Tale of Two Cities"; no doubt he found the going more difficult. The invitation to teach in California, so attractive initially, turned out to be a double disappointment: he did not get the tenured position that he deserved, and he did very little writing. This disappointment, full-time teaching, the move away from inspiring New York, and living in enervating Del Mar and Anaheim, and increasing domestic frustrations that caused him to drink heavily, combined to alienate him from the world of writing.

Though the creative urge waned considerably, it never faded away completely. To the very end, back in his beloved New York, he was revising his two unpublished novels.

Though Khan's corpus is small, it is by no means insignificant. Indeed, it comprises a unique legacy, occupying a special niche in West Indian fiction.[1] *The Jumbie Bird* (1961), based on Khan's experience of growing up in the very heart of Port of Spain with his outsized grandfather, a legend in his time, is the most serious treatment of the issue of repatriation of indentured labourers and of that crucial phase of Indo-Caribbean history.[2] His second novel, *The Obeah Man* (1964), is, as Ramchand notes, the only West Indian novel to have as its protagonist an obeah man and to treat obeah seriously, in spite of the fact that it offers no significant insights into the nature and practice of obeah.[3] *The Crucifixion* (1987) is, at least for one critic, "a finely constructed and movingly told novel, the compressed experience of the Caribbean people in search of fulfilment and freedom."[4] In this, his third and last novel, Khan has in mind C.L.R. James's two classic yard works, "Triumph" and *Minty Alley,* and, remembering his own boyhood experience of the yard at the back of his home on Frederick Street, consciously attempts to extend and expand James's narrative technique and perspective. Khan employs a hybrid narrative technique, using two competing, completing voices to create a work that is darker than James's but wider referentially. Khan's final work, *A Day in the Country & Other Stories* (1994), presents compelling scenes of country and city life in a transitional Trinidad of the 1940s and 1950s. Many stories are singular: "The Red Ball," translated into Tamil and German, and widely anthologized, shows the effects of displacement from country to city and the power of a mother/wife to negotiate a timely reconciliation between an unsympathetic father and an individualistic son, struggling for acceptance and a sense of belonging in a strange environment. "Pooran, Pooran" is perhaps the most outright condemnation in the literature of Trinidad & Tobago of the brand of colonial education offered at one the nation's leading high schools; "Shadows Move in the Britannia Bar" establishes, much more than *The Obeah Man,* the need to believe in the power of obeah and in the existence of a supersensory world; and "Shaving," oscillating between past, present, and future, shows how writing encompasses and conflates all other kinds of mirrors to become the most reflective, refractive mirror of all.

The quality and uniqueness of Khan's fiction have been recognised and praised by his reviewers and critics; the critical neglect has also been acknowledged and bemoaned. This neglect remains for Khan's critics one of the puzzles of West Indian literary criticism.[5] Perhaps Khan's deliberate preference for America, which he inherited from his anti-British father and grandfather, is partly responsible for the neglect. The vast majority of West Indian writers and critics were either living in or educated in Britain; their tendency was to look after their own. Furthermore, since there was no sizeable population of West Indian readers in America in the 1960s and 1970s; there was, unsurprisingly, little interest in West Indian literature among American publishers. (It is instructive to speculate on the difference Khan's migration to Britain would have made to the reception and assessment of his work). Perhaps, too, his Muslim and city upbringing worked against him, because it afforded him a minority perspective and experience. Perhaps, too, the critical response to Khan's fiction takes its acquiescent cue from the seminal *The West Indian Novel and Its Background* (1970), which devotes two paragraphs to *The Obeah Man*, but remains silent on *The Jumbie Bird*. Critics were simply too complacent and too willing to follow the sonorous beat of Ramchand's drum. This is not to impute any particular designs to Ramchand, for his criticism of *The Obeah Man* is balanced, though somewhat unsympathetic; rather, it is to suggest how influential this landmark work has been.[6]

II

This study, the first full-length analysis of Khan's fiction, discharges at least three important obligations.[7] In the first instance, this study fulfils a promise I made to Ismith Khan, months before he died, as we talked excitedly of my doing his biography. Sadly, he died before he could recount anything of his life. What follows in the next few lines is all that he gave in our last conversation (August 2001); it is exclusively about his paternal grandfather, Kale Khan. "He participated in the Indian Mutiny in India in 1856;

he gave away his only daughter at the Cawnpore Railway Station as he took his flight out of India; he arrived in British Guiana; came shortly after to Trinidad, settling initially in Princes Town in a small building on St Croix Road; he was a superlative jeweller, who enjoyed a widespread reputation; he carried two pistols to protect himself, his money, and his jewellery; he accidentally became a leader of the insurgents in the Hussay Riots of 1884; he moved to Port of Spain at the turn of the century, setting up the largest and most famous jewellery shop in Port of Spain; he became the self-styled leader of the wretched Indians of Woodford Square; he died in 1931." Though we kept in touch by phone and correspondence, little additional information was offered. Whatever information was given after 2001 was in response to my specific questions. Secondly, this study fulfils a self-imposed obligation of filling an obvious gap in West Indian criticism. In the critical mansion, all rooms, large and small, need to be occupied and furnished; the Khan room is, admittedly, small, but special. Finally, this study, much like my study of Selvon (2001), is a preparatory work, treating Khan's works individually, not only establishing Khan's major thematic concerns, but also analysing his structural, stylistic, and narrative strategies. Its *raison d'etre* is to encourage other studies, no doubt more specialized and searching, and to generate an ongoing critical dialogue on the fiction of Ismith Khan.

III

Using information supplied by Ismith's two younger sisters, Zuleika (New York) and Rowena (Colchester, U.K.), by Ismith's two children, Farida and Jameen, by Ismith's two former spouses, Mariam Sherar (Maine) and Vera Simone (California/China), by the companion of his last twenty years, Betty Nicholson (New York), and by Ismith himself over the years, I have put together, what I believe, is the fullest biographical sketch to date. To be sure, too much is missing to compile a biography; with Ismith gone this gap will forever remain. Those who could have helped are dead; those who are alive know too little about his early years. And to treat fictional information as historical and biographical fact is as dangerous as it is misleading. When for instance we learn that Kale Khan, his paternal grandfather died in 1931, when Ismith was only six years old, we are afforded a novel insight into his fictional strategies in *The Jumbie Bird*. For we realise that Ismith has manipulated chronology and auto/biography in keeping Kale Khan alive, as it were, propelling him into the 1940s, allowing him to meet India's first Commissioner to Trinidad, who arrived in 1948. Ismith's grandfather, and Kale Khan, Jamini's grandfather, share the identical name, but are two discrete individuals, though "not unrelated":[9] one is fact, the other largely fiction. The wonderfully dramatic airport scene (Chapter 12), the rat incident with Jamini and the official from the Ministry of Health (Chapter 11), the loveless consummation between Jamini and Lakshmi in the Lapeyrouse Cemetery (Chapter 13), Kale's final stick-fight (Chapter 13), Binti's initiative that succeeds in getting Jamini a place at Queen's Royal College (Chapter 13), Binti's exemplary behaviour at Kale's burial (Chapter 13), the housing of the family behind the coal-shop on Quarry Street (Chapter 13) are pure fiction. Not to know this is to compromise one's understanding of Khan's fictional technique in his first novel. In "Perpetual Motion", too, Khan's most autobiographical short story, we can easily be misled into believing that Ismith's father died from a stab wound he received in Woodford Square. Actually, Faiez Khan died of cardiac arrest in 1951. (Zinab, Ismith's mother, died ten years later in Trinidad, after a sojourn with her daughter in America). Yet the anonymous fictional adolescent, like Ismith, attends Queen's Royal College, and the fictional father, like Faiez Khan, is working on a machine of perpetual motion. Khan's fictional technique in *The Jumbie Bird* is as daring and complex as Naipaul's in *A House for Mr Biswas*, and Selvon's in *An Island Is A World*.

Mohamed Ismith Khan was born on March 16, 1925, in a two-storeyed building at 48 Frederick Street, facing to the west onto Woodford Square and opening out to the east onto a walled-in barrack-yard. It was in this building that he spent the first ten years of his life. His visits to the yard, though frequent, were frowned upon and discouraged by his class-conscious grandfather, who, in the role of watchman, occupied a room at the back of the largest jewellery store in Port of Spain owned latterly by Ismith's father, Faiez Khan. (His familiarity with the yard and its dwellers is evident in *The Crucifixion* and in two of his published short stories). Kale Khan, in his late eighties when Ismith was born, continued to repair jewellery, brought in by customers who believed more in his mastery of the jeweller's art than in his son's. Kale, estranged from his wife, led a very independent life downstairs, washing his clothes, cleaning his room, and cooking his food. Upstairs, Ismith lived with his mother, father and three sisters (Rowena, the youngest, was born after the family left Frederick Street). From the iron-railed, wooden gallery the family kept a close eye on activities in Woodford Square, and watched in comfort as tramcars, parades, rallies, Carnival bands, and masqueraders passed by on the street below. Woodford Square, flanked by Trinity Cathedral to the south, the Town Hall and Public Library to the north, and the Red House to the west, was in the 1930s and 1940s, as it is now, the true heart of Port of Spain. This famous city block became young Ismith's expansive playground. Here he would have seen the squalid, wretched Indians, displaced from the country and the canefields, forced by city folk to live out the root meaning of the word, "coolie"; here he would have, with makeshift bats, balls, and stumps, played cricket with his city friends; here he would have admired again and again the central fountain with its statue of Governor Woodford and its bronze mermaids; here he would spent hours catching the spiralling blossoms of the pink and yellow poui; here he would have listened weekly to the uniformed orphanage band playing from the bandstand a little northeast of the fountain; here, he would have eaten the seeds of the sweet calabash, from a tree visited at night by an invisible jumbie bird; here he would have seen and listened with childlike interest to self-styled orators, would-be politicians, and to those who felt they had something to say publicly; and here he would have spent pleasure-filled hours every Saturday morning with his grandfather, as the old man played chess, smoked his clay pipe, advising, berating, and consoling the hapless Indians.

Ismith was very close to his grandparents: indeed, in his first six years he spent more time with them than he did with his parents. He slept most week-nights in his grandfather's room, and regularly spent weekends with his grandmother. Dadi, as he affectionately called her, lived at the back of her coal and vegetable shop on Quarry

Street, a few blocks east of 48 Frederick Street. This nurturing by the grandparents gave the tender soul an early awareness of adult behaviour and an outlook that impacted somewhat on his enjoyment of childhood pleasures. Too, invariably, he became the natural human conduit of the bickering between his Dada and Dadi. He admired his flinty, domineering grandfather, but worshipped his industrious, loving grandmother. As Kale and Binti are countervailing forces in Jamini's life, so were the grandparents in Ismith's. Torn between Dada and Dadi, the young, sensitive child could not imagine life without either. Though the death of Kale, when he was six years old, was his worst childhood tragedy, it was no doubt, in an important sense, a huge relief and release. As with Jamini, young Ismith's mind was filled with notions of Pathan masculine exclusivity and of returning to Hindustan.[8] Ismith could now, under the loving tutelage of Dadi and his parents, pick up the pieces of his shattered world, and make the initial uncertain steps in the struggle for a personal identity.

Ismith began his schooling much like Jamini in *The Jumbie Bird*: he attended a private school, run by a Portuguese woman, upstairs the Empire Bar on Henry and Prince Streets. The curious boy could not help slowing down as he passed the swinging shutter-doors downstairs, taking in the sounds and aromas of the bar, and watching "from underneath the swinging half-doors the feet of the early morning customers, a few wooden halves of kegs which were used as spittoons, and the trampled sawdust around the aged kegs whose hoops had rusted, swelled, and broken away, leaving the slats quite alone, held firmly together by the encrusted layers of the substances that had settled in them through their lifetime" (*The Jumbie Bird*, p. 39). Like Bolan in "The Red Ball", Ismith attended, for a short while, Eastern Boys Government School behind the Eastern Market on George Street, Port of Spain. On his trips to and from school he would have had ample opportunity to hear and see the bustle of the busy market, sounds and sights that remained with him to the very end. In 1935, Faiez Khan gave up his jewellery store, because business had declined considerably. His clients were almost exclusively middle-class Port of Spain Indo-Trinidadians, who regularly bought expensive, heavy gold jewellery; they became more interested in saving their money to send their children abroad. The occasional patronage from tourists was not enough to keep the business going. He began to collect scrap metal, which was shipped abroad; however, wartime regulations made it impossible for him to continue in this business, as scrap metal now had to be sent to England to assist in the war effort.

Like Kemal in "A Day in the Country", Ismith was proud of the fact that he was the only one among his friends who owned a bicycle. Though the parents were protective of their only son, they gave him liberties denied to the older sisters. He was allowed to come home late after school every day. His bicycle took him regularly to the La Basse to meet Peter, who collected scrap metal for his father. While at the La Basse, Ismith rode through every dusty track that separated the squalid shanties on the city dump. This familiarity with the city dump forms the basis of the cogency of the setting of the abodes of Massahood, Hop and Drop, and Zolda in *The Obeah Man*. His bicycle, which he ritually disassembled and reassembled, took him, not only to Queen's Royal College daily, a few minutes from home, but also much farther on weekends to Carenage and to the Blue Basin waterfall on the lower reaches on the Northern Range. This famous spot of surpassing natural beauty is chosen by Khan in his second novel to be the home of Zampi, the obeah man. There was not a part of the city that young Ismith did not know. This familiarity with the capital and its environs is everywhere evident in his fiction; his setting is as authentic as one can imagine. Indeed no other author has written so lovingly and tellingly of Port of Spain and its outskirts; Khan is pre-eminently the novelist of the capital city.

The family, who did not own the building at 48 Frederick Street, moved to another rented house at 55 Richmond Street, a stone's throw from Richmond Boys E.C. School, where Ismith enrolled and completed his primary school education. Both parents were committed to providing the best education for Ismith and his sisters, who initially attended the Sacred Heart School, run by local nuns, and later, Tranquillity. Ismith was a bright student, topping his class regularly; his academic standing and his parents' ability to afford the tuition fees are what got him a place at Queen's Royal College, and not the intercession of his Dadi, as we might deduce from *The Jumbie Bird*. Ismith entered Queen's Royal College as a student of Form 3B in September 1939. Initially out of place among the majority of non-Indo-Trinidadians from privileged middle-class homes, Ismith never really settled in comfortably. This inability to settle in is perhaps evident from his lacklustre academic performance. The school's records show that Ismith was awarded a Grade III in the Cambridge School Certificate, gaining distinctions in oral Spanish and oral French, largely because of the tutors who came to his home. He passed Spanish, French, English, Mathematics, Hygiene, and Physics. The most curiously ironic detail of his certificate is his failure in English Literature! His Grade III did not allow him to proceed to the Higher School Certificate. After five years and an undistinguished academic record, he left Queen's Royal College in 1945.

On graduating from Queen's Royal College, Ismith did several odd jobs. In 1947 he left for the University of Indiana at Fort Wayne to study engineering, acquiescing in his father's hope that he would become an engineer. Fortunately for West Indian literature, Ismith's money ran out after the first year. He returned to Trinidad in 1948, and encouraged by Samuel Selvon, joined him on the staff of the *Trinidad Guardian*, the nation's leading newspaper. He had met Selvon in 1941, at the wedding of Dennis (Selvon's older brother), and Betty, (Ismith's older sister). Though the marriage did not last long, Ismith and Selvon became lifelong friends. Selvon was a frequent visitor to 55 Abercromby Street, developing a passing romantic interest in Ismith's beautiful younger sister, Zuleika. Selvon's visits stopped when he joined the Royal Navy, but he corresponded regularly with Ismith and the family. When Selvon's stint with the navy was over, he returned to Trinidad and began working with the *Trinidad Guardian*. Within months, he had begun to write and had published in the *Trinidad Guardian* and the *Guardian Weekly* several short stories, poems, and non-fiction pieces; unlike Ismith, he knew that he wanted to become a writer. It was at this time that the two men cemented their friendship. Daily, the two friends spent a lot of time after work, especially at the popular Britannia Bar (at the eastern corner of Broadway and South Quay, opposite the train terminal), smoking, drinking, and chatting about Sam's stories and poems. Though he began writing many years later it was at this time that Ismith began to develop an interest in writing and to sense that he, too, could become a writer. His friendship with Selvon, his closest lifelong friend, he confessed, was the single most powerful influence in his becoming a writer.

While at the *Trinidad Guardian*, Ismith was sent to interview a young American student, Mariam Ghose, the daughter of a pre-Gandhian revolutionary, who came to Trinidad to finish a project for her degree in social anthropology from Michigan State University. The two quickly became friends, and she was a frequent visitor to 55 Abercromby Street. She encouraged Ismith to apply for a tuition scholarship to her university, and in the fall of 1948, he left Trinidad on a scholarship. Though he spent the next four years in the sociology programme at Michigan State University, he did not take a degree, as he refused to fulfil the institution's requirement of taking a course in physical education. Through Mariam's agency, he was offered a scholarship to The New School For Social Research in New York, where he eventually obtained a degree in sociology. Frequent correspondence from Selvon, who left Trinidad for London in 1950, and a course in creative writing at the New School for Social Research was the combined catalyst in his becoming a writer. His submissions for the course showed promise, and his tutor encouraged him. He wrote much more than was required; writing was now in his blood. Selvon and his tutor gave him the same advice: "Write about what you know most." While working at the New York Public Library in Manhattan, Ismith began work on his first novel. On Friday evenings after work, he spent hours at the Peacock Restaurant and the Figaro Bar in Greenwich Village, scribbling away with ballpoint and pencil on cheap yellow sheets. At home, Mariam, whom he married in 1949, always ready with words of encouragement, happily typed these pages. She also worked at two jobs to give Ismith as much time as he needed to write. It was at these two establishments that Ismith wrote *The Jumbie Bird*, *The Obeah Man*, and the majority of his short stories. This was the most productive phase of Ismith's writing career.

At a party organised by colleagues at Queen's College in 1964, at Mariam's apartment, Ismith first met Vera Reichler (nee Simon). Vera, drawn fatefully to the flamenco music of Ismith's guitar from a back room, was entranced by "the most enchanting man I have ever known" (Vera's email of March 26, 2007). A year later, they began a love affair, and in 1966, he moved in with her to her Bedford Street apartment. This apartment proved too small, and they moved to a railroad flat at 72 Charles Street, where they, in the first flush of romance, spent their happiest times. It was here that Ismith began writing *The Crucifixion*, while Vera worked on *China in Revolution* (1968), an edited paperback. Ismith divorced Mariam in October 1968, and married Vera on January 03, 1969. In the fall of 1969, Ismith and Vera left New York for Baltimore, where Ismith, on the invitation of Elliott Coleman, the head of the writing programme, enrolled in the Master's degree in Creative Writing at the Johns Hopkins University. In May 1970, Ismith completed the Master's degree in Fine Arts, submitting *The Crucifixion* as his thesis. After a summer in Europe, when they stayed with Selvon and his wife, Althea, in London, and visited France, Spain, and Italy, Vera and Ismith moved in the fall of 1970 to the University of California at Berkeley, where Ismith met, among others, Mark Schorer and Seamus Heaney, two of his colleagues. The protracted discussions about literary matters, with the well-known American critic and the Irish writer (1995 Nobel Prize winner), whetted Ismith's appetite for a full-time career as an academic. In 1971, Ismith was offered an assistant professorship at the Third College of the University of San Diego in La Jolla, where he spent the next three years in anticipation of a tenured position. Full-time teaching, "serious socialising" (Vera's email), and compulsive fishing left him little time for writing, though he completed 215 pages of a novel, tentatively entitled "A Tale of Two Cities". During his stay at UCSD, Vera and Ismith frequented Mexico, making Puerto Vallarta their favourite haunt. In 1975, Vera and Ismith adopted a six-month-old Guamanian baby, whom they named Jameen (after Jamini in *The Jumbie Bird*); this filled a void in Vera's life. Though family life was fulfilling, Ismith regretted that Vera was spending less time with him and more with Jameen. In 1978, Ismith taught creative writing first at Long Beach, then at the University of Southern California, where he met Lloyd Brown, who became deeply interested in Ismith's work. Disappointed that he was passed over for tenure, frustrated that he was writing so little, and resentful of Vera's visits to China, Ismith found refuge in the bottle. Predictably, family life was adversely affected; the marriage became, to use Vera's words, "increasingly prickly with each of us disappointed in the other." When Vera stopped drinking altogether, Ismith interpreted this as another withdrawal on her part. He drank more heavily.

Unable to cope with life in South Clementine, Anaheim, Ismith left Vera and Jameen, and returned to New York in 1981, with a serious drinking problem. Mariam, who remarried in 1969, and with whom he had stayed in touch, picked up a changed former husband at the JFK Airport. She hardly recognised Ismith: he was drunk and shabbily dressed. He continued to drink heavily, and became very depressed. Mariam, who never stopped loving him, did as much as she could for him. She found a room for him at the Hotel St George in Brooklyn, visited him often there, invited him over to her apartment, and consoled him. Saddened by his transformation, she convinced him that he needed professional help. At an Alcoholics Anonymous meeting in 1981, he met Betty Nicholson. In 1982 he divorced Vera, and in the same year he moved into Betty's apartment at 26 Eastern Parkway, where he remained until he died. In 1986, he was offered a job at Medgar Evers College to teach English I and English II; his fifteen years of teaching at Medgar Evers College (1986-2001) brought him tremendous satisfaction; he was well respected by his colleagues and adored by his students, many of whom were of West Indian descent. Betty, inclined to writing herself, began introducing herself to Ismith's writing. She was fascinated by the whole new world that Ismith's fiction opened up to her, the world of Trinidadian (and West Indian) life, with its peculiar history, sights, sounds, colours, and contradictions. Emotionally, she readily entered and embraced his fictional world. She encouraged him to continue his writing; he began revising "A Tale of Two Cities" and "In Search of Stella", a novel based in New York begun during his most productive phase.

IV

Like Selvon, Ismith was a chain smoker for the better part of his adult life, and a moderate-to-heavy drinker. Like Selvon, too, he never cared for premium scotch or aged rums, preferring the younger, harsher taste of Johnny Walker Red, Teachers, and Vat 19. During my last visit with him at 26 Eastern Parkway, Brooklyn, he sent me out on a windy August day to a nearby liquor mart to buy a bottle of Johnny Walker Red; over the following two days, I tried to accustom myself to this new, harsh experience. Ismith's company, though, made it palatable. In the Caribbean, more often than not, he drank rum; I cannot remember him using ice or chaser in his scotch and rum. Like Selvon, too, there was so much of the connoisseur in him. He loved to fish and to cook, and prided himself on being a chef, able to please the palate of all his guests, whether Mexican, Indian, West Indian, or American. Vera's anecdote indicates not only his connoisseurship but also his perfectionism in the kitchen: "In the process of making stuffed artichokes, the top part of the artichoke has to be removed to fill the spaces between the leaves with garlic, anchovies and spices. When I cut the artichoke so that its top (when served) was slanted, Ismith's reproach was like a bolt out of Heaven." He enjoyed a variety of food, some of which is considered haram by Muslims, a fact that did not cause him concern. He had, like so many of his characters, a special fondness for black pudding (blood sausage); the best pudding, he repeatedly said, was from a vendor in St Helena, a stone's throw from the Piarco airport. On his last visit to Trinidad, he insisted that we go to St Helena; the vendor was a different one, but the pudding was still excellent, he confessed. And he cooked for my family a splendid rack of baby-back ribs, drenched in a honey-soy sauce, the recipe for which I have tried many times. He had, like Hop and Drop, a Trinidadian zest for raw oysters, avoiding the cocktail, and preferring to drink from the shell of a freshly opened oyster. Though he did not care for Indian sweets, except gulab jamoon, he was fond of the savoury saheena and kachourie. In spite of his long stay abroad, he never lost his predilection for mangoes, especially those grown in Trinidad. Whenever available, he especially enjoyed curried cascadoo and curried crab, two dishes popular among Indo-Trinidadians.

Though Muslim by birth and upbringing, (he and his family regularly attended the "mosque" in St Joseph – a few hundred yards north east of the present Jinnah Memorial Mosque – when he was a boy), he did not as an adult adhere to Muslim teaching or practices. He was more influenced by his father, who smoked and drank, than by his deeply religious mother, who daily read the Koran. Though Ismith was not religious, he was a spiritual man. No doubt influenced first by his famous iconoclastic grandfather and then by his free-thinking father, Ismith grew increasingly wary of man-made systems. Religion, to him, was a man-made system, more divisive than unifying. He never argued about religion, showing an admirable tolerance for the religious beliefs of others. He was a soft-spoken, avuncular man, who was a model listener, as he smoked and drank his neat liquor. Like Selvon, though somewhat more reserved, he was a humble man, who never lost his Trinidadian-ness, even though he had spent over fifty years in the United States. He was a good social mixer, moving easily from surprisingly long chats with my Down-syndrome brother, to addressing high-school students, rapt and eager, to holding his own from the podium at a conference or lecture, to simply being one of the boys at a river lime. (I remember when Ismith and his daughter, Farida, accompanied my friends and me to Caura River on a rainy day. I can still picture Ismith, with glass in hand expressing his gratitude for being able to enjoy one of the simple things in life, and Farida, all smiles, on her bottom, having slipped on the muddy slope!). His early nurture with Dada and Dadi allowed him to have a special relationship with my octogenarian mother, who, herself from Muslim stock, no doubt reminded him of the grandmother he worshipped. Lacking Selvon's penchant for "picong" (abrasive repartee), he nevertheless revelled in a good joke. He often used this anecdote to define the Trinidadian sense of humour: "An accused was asked by the magistrate why he stole the cow. The accused replied that he stole a rope, and when he went home he found a cow at the end of it. To take back the cow would have make his guilt obvious. He decided to keep both rope and cow. He insisted that he be charged for stealing only the rope." He had catholic tastes in food and music: he played a "passionate, resolute flamenco guitar",[10] possessed a good library of vintage calypsos, enjoyed the twang of country music, and often relaxed while listening to the classical masters. A few abstract charcoal canvases, which hang on Mariam's wall in Maine, done in his most productive phase, round off an admirable artistic versatility.

Ismith's heavy smoking and drinking, his high salt intake (he invariably added a pinch of salt to his food before tasting it; this was a Khan family habit), the nagging disappointment over the neglect of his work by critics, and the knowledge that he could have accom-plished more, took their toll on his health. Betty Nicholson, who shared the last twenty years of his life at 26 Eastern Parkway, Brooklyn, gives this account of his last days: "He began to show symptoms of his illness which was finally diagnosed as a form of Parkinson's Disease about three years ago. It was a very slow degen-eration of movement and speech and for a man for whom talking and writing were as essential as breathing it was a particularly cruel burden. Towards the end his speech was so difficult and frustrating, he just stopped trying. Out of pride he refused to talk on the phone.

His hands developed a tremor and were eventually too weak to use a processor or even to write in long hand, nor, because of his speech impediment could he dictate to me or a tape recorder… Locked in himself as he was, he must have been unbearably lonely… About an hour before he unexpectedly and suddenly died of a heart attack, his last improbable words were, "You does find Cascadura in the market?"[11]

In June 2002, a memorial service for Ismith was held at the St Joseph Mosque. Relatives, some of whom still live in St Joseph, and friends spoke lovingly and proudly of this humble, city-born Trinidadian who had migrated and become a well-known writer. There were personal reminiscences from those who grew up with him, and a moment of silence was observed. I read a short story, (still unpublished and dedicated to his memory) based on a real-life incident, about an old woman and a jumbie bird that came one morning to the Buxton Spice mango tree that overlooks my patio in Caiman Road, St Joseph, a quarter mile north of the mosque. It was a rare experience for my mother and me; few Trinidadians have seen or can recognise a jumbie bird. Ismith, I am sure, would have savoured our experience. On the day following the memorial service, Betty Nicholson and I first drove to UWI, St Augustine, where she scattered some of Ismith's ashes on Selvon's grave; a hour or so later, while I waited in the car in front of a no-parking sign almost directly opposite 48 Frederick Street, Betty scattered ashes in Woodford Square, his childhood playground; finally, we drove to Carenage, where he and his truant, boyhood friends swam regularly. Betty pensively emptied the remaining ashes in the placid, shallow water. Ismith, like Selvon, harkening to the indwelling call of the loricate cascadura, had finally returned home. Though his voice and pen have been forever stilled, from the pages of his singular literary legacy, his quiet, unassuming voice speaks in its authentic tone and style, defining a unique, personal vision of West Indian man.

Notes

1. Lloyd Brown, "Ismith Khan", *Contemporary Novelists* (New York: St Martins Press, 1982), p. 497.
2. Arthur Drayton, "Ismith Khan", *Fifty Caribbean Writers: A Bio-Bibliographical Critical Sourcebook*. Ed. Daryl Cumber Dance (Connecticut: Greenwood Press, 1986), p. 248.
3. Kenneth Ramchand, "Obeah and the Supernatural in West Indian Literature," *Jamaica Journal* 3: 2 (June 1969): 52-54. These two paragraphs are reprised verbatim in *The West Indian Novel and Its Background* (1970, 1983).
4. Chris Searle, "Lives in the yard: *The Crucifixion*." Review of *The Crucifixion*. <www. peepaltreepress.com/review display .asp? rev. id=87>
5. Lloyd Brown, Rhonda Cobham, and Arthur Drayton, who together have written most on Ismith Khan, lament this neglect. Brown speaks of "the curiously neglected novels of Ismith Khan ("The Isolated Self in West Indian Literature,"p. 60) while Cobham berates the "somewhat myopic Caribbean or Commonwealth scholars," and concludes that there "seems no valid reason for his neglect" (*"The Jumbie Bird*: A New Assessment," p. 240).
6. It is unfortunate that the expanded edition (2004) of this landmark work omits the crucial paragraphs on *The Obeah Man*, though it contains a passing reference to *The Obeah Man* and *The Jumbie Bird* in a chapter on *The Dragon Can't Dance* (174). As the expanded edition replaces the older editions (1970, 1983), as it must, readers will erroneously deduce that Ramchand has nothing to say about Khan's fiction. Indeed, readers will be happy to know that Ramchand discusses Khan's fiction, especially *The Jumbie Bird*, in three of his weekly columns in the *Trinidad Guardian* ("Matters Arising," May 11, 19, 25, 1988).
7. To date, there are four encyclopedia entries and only three articles totally devoted to Khan's works (Cobham, Juneva, and Lacovia); two of these (Cobham and Juneva) deal exclusively with *The Jumbie Bird*, and the other includes *The Obeah Man* in its analysis. My introduction to the reprint (TSAR, 1995) is the only essay wholly devoted to *The Obeah Man*. Only a

few reviews have appeared on *The Crucifixion* and *A Day in the Country & Other Stories.*

8. The Hindustan that Kale Khan speaks of refers to an India that remembers its emigrés and is eager to welcome them back. Such an India, as the Commissioner reminds us, no longer exists. Hindustan was the popular name for the pre-independence, pre-partition geographic region of the sub-continent. This Hindustan is not to be confused with the well-known Trinidadian village that is the home to mud volcanoes, a few miles south-east of Princes Town.

9. Arthur Drayton, "Ismith Khan", *Fifty Caribbean Writers: A Bio-bibliographical Critical Sourcebook*, p. 247.

10. Betty Nicholson, "Call of the Cascadura" (2003), p. 10. This is Betty Nicholson's unpublished, personal "eulogy" for Ismith.

11. Nicholson, p. 14.

CHAPTER ONE

THE JUMBIE BIRD

I

Ismith Khan's first novel, *The Jumbie Bird* (1961), was initially published in England by MacGibbon & Kee and, in 1962, simultaneously by Ivan Obolensky of New York and George J. Mcleod of Toronto. Samuel Selvon, Khan's relative by marriage and closest lifelong friend,[1] had published *Ways of Sunlight* (1957) and *Turn Again Tiger* (1958) with MacGibbon & Kee, and it was he who encouraged Khan and his agent, John Schaffner, to send his manuscript to the London-based publishers. The quality of the manuscript was such that there was no need for any intercession by the more established writer.[2] Somewhat like Selvon's first novel, *A Brighter Sun* (1952), *The Jumbie Bird* is semi-autobiographical, fictionalising two to three years in the life of the Khan family.[3] But we need always to be wary, as Stewart Brown reminds us, of confusing fiction with fact.[4] Khan has confessed, to Drayton and others, that the demands of his fiction forced him to represent his father as someone weak and indecisive, quite different from what he was in real life.[5] And if we assume, with Deborah John, that Jamini is a version of the young Ismith, we are to some extent correct.[6] However, if we accept as factual the chronology of the novel, which ends in 1948,[7] with the coming out of India's first Commissioner to the Caribbean, and recall that Ismith was born in 1925, then we have the odd situation of Jamini being admitted to Queen's Royal College, the island's oldest non-denominational high school, at the age of 23! Furthermore, we are told that Jamini at the beginning of the narrative is twelve years old (p. 44). Yet Khan's development as a young boy living at 48 Frederick Street, across from the most famous square in Trinidad, and growing up under the loving, watchful eyes of his grandmother and in the shadow of his grandfather, who many years before had made a name for himself as jeweller, stickfighter, and rebel against colonial authority, is the experiential quarry from which the *The Jumbie Bird* is fashioned. Khan consciously adapts and manipulates auto/biography to suit the exigencies of his most important and well-known novel.[8] And as the Introduction to this volume makes clear, there is much more creative fictionalising than we assume.

The extra-narrative prologue introduces the eponymous bird, and drawing upon folklore, enhances the fictional stature of the jumbie bird. Trinidadian folklore simply maintains that the jumbie bird is a harbinger of death, and recognises that it is nocturnal and rarely seen. Of course, this quasi-invisibility serves to increase its putative mystery and power. Khan goes beyond these simple folkloric beliefs and invests his titular bird with more extensive powers befitting a deity. For the jumbie bird not only is given power over man but also has the ability to "blacken the moon", to darken the night, causing the moon to duck behind the clouds (p. xviii).[9] Khan goes further by first establishing the pedigree of the jumbie bird: "the bastard child of the devil" and a "whore" (p. xvii). Unlike the god of death of classical mythology, who is neither good nor evil, the jumbie bird is "evil", formed from the droppings of devils (p. xviii). Instead of ichor, the vital ethereal fluid of the Greek gods, Khan has "the bitter gall of rubbed cucumber edges flow[ing] in [its] poisonous veins" (p. xviii).[10] Using inflation and deflation, Khan creates an ambiguous avian character, whose control is arbitrary and imagined, a threat only to those who believe in its mortiferous powers. Rahim, Meena, and Jamini, among others, are afraid of the jumbie bird; neither Binti nor Kale is. Indeed, Kale, the male protagonist for the greater part of the narrative, has no relationship whatever with the titular bird, and Binti, in a pivotal scene, defies the jumbie bird and puts it to flight.

The jumbie-bird, which is rarely seen, and whose habits are known only to the most thoroughgoing ornithologist, is presented in this novel as a combination of the classical Fates and Nemesis. It neither spins nor determines the quality of life, as Clotho does, but like Lachesis and Atropos, it measures and cuts the fragile yarn of life. And in Jamini's and Rahim's internalisation of island folklore (pp. 126, 142), the jumbie bird has the power of retribution: "An old man once threw a stone at the jumbie bird and the next day he died on the Town Hall steps" (p. xviii). Khan takes further risks by choosing to establish the colour, size, and voice of the jumbie bird: he gives it "black feathers" (p. xviii), "large wings" (122), and a call of "twee-twee-twee" (p. xviii). All of which, surprisingly, he gets wrong, though his description of the "keskidee" (*pitangus sulphuratus*) is very accurate (pp. 163-4). Richard ffrench's highly-acclaimed *A Guide to the Birds of Trinidad & Tobago* establishes that the jumbie bird is the most diminutive of owls, and although it is listed as the ferruginous (rust-coloured) pygmy owl, it is generally brown with white spots on the crown and wing coverts, and utters a regular series of musical hoots of "wup-wup-wup" or "chirrup-chirrup-chirrup".[11] Khan's jumbie bird, then, unlike Shakespeare's croaking raven that calls out Duncan's fateful entrance into Macbeth's castle, is a product of pure imagination and folklore. It is reasonable to assume, therefore, that Khan never, as boy or adult, saw or heard a real-life jumbie bird, or if he did, was unable to recall its true appearance and call. But then again few Trinidadians have. It is perhaps worth mentioning that a species of jumbie bird (*glaucidium brasilianum phaloenides*) is found only in Trinidad.[12] This helps to locate Khan's narrative specifically in Trinidad, his native land, rather than in the Caribbean at large. Since the titular bird does not impact significantly on the unfolding of the narrative,[13] it is tempting to suggest that Khan chose his title because he wanted to present a specifically Trinidadian experience of a unique family, whose life is meant in some ways to be exemplary. Following Selvon, especially in his peasant novels and the middle-class novels, and Naipaul, in his early Trinidad-based stories and novels, Khan, in *The Jumbie Bird*, *The Obeah Man*, *The Crucifixion*, and his short stories, seeks to put Trinidad on the literary map.

The inclusion of a "Prologue" suggests a structural framework, but there is no matching epilogue, so entitled. Yet, there is an epilogue, especially if we consider Binti's ascendancy (pp. 182-190) a fitting counterbalance to Kale's egomania and to the implacability of the jumbie bird. Binti's protective dominance within the family virtually drives away, for a time, both the jumbie bird and thoughts and the fear of death. The natural, quiet morning sounds of the matriarch looking after her reunited family replace the ominous nocturnal squawking of the jumbie bird (p. 184). Her defiance of the bird (p. 125), her refusal to feel afraid in the presence of death, and her willingness to descend into Kale's waterlogged grave (p. 180), combine to give her a stature at the end that clearly overshadows that of Kale and that of the jumbie bird. The prologue centres the jumbie bird; most of the middle section celebrates the exploits of Kale; and the epilogue eulogises Binti.

The narrative proper (pp. 1-190), set against a backdrop of changing seasons and the celebration of a central Muslim festival, creolised and carnivalised, can be divided into two unequal sections. The first section (pp. 1-1st par. 171) is eight times the length of the second (pp. 171-190). The first is devoted to the life and death of Kale; the second, to the emergence of Binti as a true matriarch. As attractive and necessary as Kale's outsized heroism has been, Binti's quiet, understated heroism is more balanced and contemporary. Kale is a retrograde hero; Binti, a future-oriented hero(ine), who assumes Kale's mantle and knits up the family fabric that Kale uncaringly ravels. Hers is the ability without fanfare or grandstanding to take complete charge of a divided, broken family, and to create for them a fecund matrix for rejuvenation, to offer each member new hope for meaningful life. What Kale divides and kills, she reunites and resuscitates; what he rejects and denies, she embodies and endorses; where he fails in his grandiose scheme of repatriation, she succeeds in giving the family a new home, new life, and a new homeland.

II

The larger section of the narrative proper commences with the sound of Kale's iron walking-stick rapping on the landing of the stairs, as he awakens at his convenience the sleeping family upstairs, forcing them to live by his arbitrary sleeping and waking habits. This initial association with metal and rapping suggests a hard, flinty outlook, unresponsive to human feeling. Such a reading appears to be reinforced by his "bright metallic grey hair cut short, looking like a spinning ball" (p. 3). And there is surely something caricatural in his "four or five blackened teeth showing between thin dry lips, and large ears sticking out" (p. 3). This technique of combined inflation and deflation points to the essential irony in Khan's characterisation of both the jumbie bird and of Kale. Kale awakens the family at his convenience because he is a tyrant, and because his "shrunken body" (p. 3), wracked by pains and cramps, needs its regular massaging from Rahim. Though his strength has waned, he is by no means decrepit or helpless. Indeed, he still can marshal, seemingly at will, admirable strength and courage. He is the oldest family member and in all probability the oldest in the Indian community. The years, to be sure, have taken their toll, particularly on the body, but his mind is still alert and discerning. With the natural weakening of his body comes the gradual strengthening of his mind and spirit. For the senescent Pathan, the power of the gun and lathi gives way to the sway of the spoken and written word. His association with crafting jewellery, with the mastery of the stickfighter's art, with arousing the masses by the power of his spoken word, and with writing letters, moulds him into an artist figure of sorts, pointing the way to others, decoding the "Obeah" (p. 90) of colonial government, and enjoying a self-imposed isolation.[14]

Early in the narrative, Kale is introduced as an old man, evidently in his eighties, caught in a time warp, who believes that he is still a member of the Royal Pathan Regiment of Her Majesty (p. 8). He lives life as if it were an ongoing military campaign. Consequently, he prepares himself meticulously for daily skirmishes. His otherwise respectful daughter-in-law, Meena, laughs behind his back at his practice of sleeping on a straight, flat board, an old signboard with its advertisements rubbed off, looking like an old faded picture (p. 2). He is not "a rigid artefact," as Cobham argues (p. 244); such a reductionist reading unnecessarily dehumanises a vibrant, spirited character. Rather, there is something decidedly surreal and stylised about the old warrior; and in the "incongruous jigsaw puzzle of large colourful cinema posters" with "their incomplete words" (p. 5) that adorn the walls of his room, there is a strong metonymic suggestion of celluloid self-aggrandisement, of wishing to be associated with, or seeing himself as one of the high-riding heroes of the silver screen. Khan, once more, leaves little doubt about the ambivalence of his characterisation: there is something "incongruous" and "incomplete" and unfulfilled about Kale. Meena also resents his constant shouting in a voice, which to her, is "cold, and hard, and filled with anger" (p. 9); and his customary angry tones indicate that he does not care or know how to express gratitude. Much of his attitude and behaviour irritates and amuses his daughter-in-law, who is not afraid to let her husband know how she feels about the old man. It is not just that he is old-fashioned in the worst way; rather, it is because he is a divisive influence in her family, wilfully creating a rift between her and her only son, as he had done years before when he had taken Rahim away from Binti, not allowing the mother to visit her only son (p. 9). We find Meena at the end of her emotional tether, speaking out in desperation to a husband, too weak to stand up to the tyrant. Kale is initially introduced as well as a man of hates: indeed, hatred for just about everything characterises his world view and his attendant behaviour: "... he hated beds, he hated women, he hated women's hands touching his clothes, his food. He hated India ... he hated Trinidad" (p. 2). This consumptive hatred of things outside of himself makes him a consummate egotist, which is at once his strength and his weakness.[15] It makes him heroic in the eyes of his followers and disciples, especially of his grandson, yet it makes him look silly in the eyes of Binti and Meena. The masculine world lionises and adulates him; the feminine world deprecates and scoffs at his myopic chauvinism.

Although we learn that at his age he is a man who walked the night with no-one, that he saw the world and kept it to himself (p. 3), we sense that very early in his life he became a loner and a rebel. The life of the masculine rebel in this novel is a lonely life. His aloneness creates a behaviour that is arbitrary and uncompromising, evidenced when he ran away with Binti, (the cause for which is never given in the novel), gave away their only daughter, according to Meena "to a total stranger" (p. 10) at the Cawnpore Railway Station, and left India. His egotism, not surprisingly, makes him a jealous husband, who in Princes Town (the first place he settled in Trinidad) early in his marriage "built a barricaded walk to keep [Binti] to himself, and did not want the eyes of other men cast upon her face" (p. 37). It may be argued in Kale's defence that this is accepted Muslim practice, but nothing in the novel, except his name, tells us that he is Muslim, and his belligerent atheism (p. 70) speaks volumes against any defence. Binti, swept away by the romance of it all, was happy in the spring-time of her marriage and did not object to being treated as a piece of her husband's filigree jewellery. Added to this, the callous dereliction of his daughter never seems to bother Kale, and Khan does not permit him at any time remorse or compunction. It is the first instance of his Pathan misogyny, and we are not surprised to learn that he has discarded Binti, and has nothing really to do with Meena. But Khan deepens his ambivalent portrait of Kale by showing that he is capable of affection and tenderness towards Lakshmi, when he meets her at home on the evening of Empire Day (pp. 50-52), and especially towards Jamini, "in whom the whole universe of his Dada's life had come to centre, to find its one reward" (p. 11). Children, it appears, are not among his manifold hatreds. The two most significant children in the narrative humanise the hard old man, eliciting, without reluctance or stint, his softest, gentlest utterances and gestures.

Yet his egomania brings him his finest moments of heroism; somewhat like the jumbie bird, there is a mythology associated with his name, as Jamini boasts to Lakshmi (p. 50). During the Hussay Riots of 1884, he first establishes his credentials as the finest stickfighter in Princes Town, then emerges, by accident, as the leader of the Indians when he takes command in his celebrated retaliation against the mounted police and armed officers. The serio-comic incident starts off innocently enough when "a little boy of about five", eluding his mother's grip, challenges Kale by waving a lathi, causing the stickfighter's face to burst "into a sea of laughter" (p. 81). Laughter dramatically turns to tragedy as the mother is killed by the mounted policeman's violent blow to the small of her back and the little boy is crushed to death by the policeman's falling horse. As the officers open fire on the defenceless crowd of men, women, and children, Kale instinctively becomes the Pathan military commander, taking charge and issuing specific orders to his fellow Indians to distribute guns and for each "to pick out one man" (p. 81). This is the moment he has prepared himself for, and he rises to the occasion. He leads by fearless example, and his flying lathi finds its mark in the face of an officer with a bright red moustache, knocking him off his horse to become the easy kill of irate, turbulent Indians. Oblivious to the pain of the gunshot wound in his thigh, he stands tall and proud as the bugle sounds retreat. This is a defining moment for Kale as his exploits in the Hussay Riots transform him into the acknowledged leader of the Indian community. His mastery of the jeweller's art had brought him a high reputation; suddenly he is catapulted into the

limelight. His reputation as jeweller, stickfighter, and rebel earns him
a sure niche in the Indian community and a place in the authentic
history of Trinidad. Like most true leaders, Kale is conscious that he is
creating history, as he boasts to his co-rebels in the thick of the fray: "
. . . let we give them a fight they go remember when they write the
history of Trinidad" (p. 81). Much earlier in the narrative, Kale, in a
conversation with Mongroo and Kareem, alerts his countrymen to the
difference between colonialist history and history as it actually happened (p. 16). To the Indian Commissioner, Kale gives his version of
the complete history of indentured Indians in Trinidad (p. 158). Khan,
it is clear, has given to his male protagonist the author's need to create
an alternative history: " ...the writer from the Caribbean has to assume
the responsibility of 'teacher' and 'historian' in order to record periods
of history, not normally found in history books."[16] Yet Khan makes it
clear that Kale understands neither the complexity nor the implications of the historical process in which he participates.[17]

His reputation follows him when he leaves Princes Town in the
south and moves to the capital in the north. He has made a distinctive
mark in the south, now he has come to leave a similar mark in the
north. This move from south to north ensures that his reputation
spreads "from one end of the island to the other" (pp. 165-6). No
longer young and energetic, he nevertheless maintains his egotism in
Port of Spain and basks in the lambent light of adulation from the
doubly-displaced Indians. Deracinated initially from Hindustan and
latterly from the sugar-cane fields, these decrepit, homeless Indians
lead squalid lives in the uncompanionable city, making Woodford
Square their home. Khan underscores the tragic irony that stymies
the lives of these formerly indentured labourers. They leave the
demanding canefields only to be forced once more to live out the root
meaning of the word "coolie"; "...they waited for someone to come
by and pay them three or four cents to carry heavy loads and bundles,
which seemed to [be] the chief source of commerce that the perpetual residents of Woodford Square carried on... " (p. 21). Betrayed
by the colonial masters, despised by contemptuous urban folk, shorn
of dignity, stoned by boys, and hounded by policemen, they look to
Kale as their spokesman, advocate, and saviour. He is their only hope
in this new land. He assumes the role with pride and relish, and
savours every moment, playing chess in Woodford Square, and
meticulously preparing himself mentally and physically for the final

encounter. His preparation is deliberate and well orchestrated. He parleys his obsession with returning to Hindustan into a passion with which he rouses and moulds the consciousness of the Indians. He passes on to the wretched Indians his detestation of the British and their dehumanisation of his compatriots. He anticipates their burgeoning resolve by taking the initiative to write a letter to the Governor; and he never fails to remind all of the duplicity of Empire Day, a day that celebrates for him the paramount need for and authority of colonialists, a day when the drab Town Hall is transformed into something with a fairyland quality by red, white, and blue lights, a day for most to enjoy a welcome respite from a soul-destroying tedium. While Rahim, Meena, and others appear to revel in the festive paraphernalia of colonial sovereignty, Kale refuses to join them or be duped by the gaudy reminder of conquest, betrayal, and servitude.

Though Kale speaks of "we" (pp. 64, 66), and no doubt has the interests of his fellow Indians somewhat at heart, it is clear that he is primarily for himself as he instructs Jamini, "Nobody ain't give you nuttin' in this world, you have to make everything you-self" (p. 70). Too, his conscious superiority as a Pathan makes it impossible for him to care genuinely for the ex-indentured labourers, who, for him, are "low-class coolies in bond" (p. 3). Ever cognisant of his name and fame, and of his position among his fellow Indians and aware of his superiority as a Pathan, he, conscious that he is participating in the creating of history, continues to carve out a niche by himself, for himself. Convinced that government, as he experiences it, is colonialism at its worst because it dehumanises Indians (p. 92), he carefully plans his countermoves. He reads the newspapers regularly, organises a meeting in Woodford Square, and travels across the island preaching his message of the need to return to Hindustan, and insisting that learning to read and write is a prerequisite to repatriation. All, especially the children, he insists, must "read the history of [their] own people" (p. 152).   He is the only one in the novel who understands just how duplicitous language, especially that of the coloniser, is.[18] His reputation mushrooms, and he becomes to his own generation and a new generation a legend, an outsized figure. To the police and government officials, however, he becomes an intractable problem:

At Police Headquarters and Government House, his name was on the tongues of all. They wondered why they had not done away with this little sprig of a man long ago, for now it was too late, now they would have to answer to one hundred and eighty thousand Indians and the resentments of one hundred years of deprivation and abuse simmering on the surface, which required only the faintest spark to explode into a horrible nightmare. (p. 153)

Kale also prepares himself physically for the final showdown. He receives a daily massage; revitalises his waning strength and aching body with white carrots,[19] bones "with plenty marrow inside" (p. 145), gold-coloured mustard seed which he germinates in the white carrots, and pink-snail broth which he consumes every other day. He completes his regimen with a bottle of cod liver oil, from which he drinks liberally. Having no use for lawyers or doctors, typified by Salwan and Gopal, respectively, or for professionals, he is his own best physician, for his transformation is nothing short of dramatic:

Kale Khan's face, his actions, his voice all livened. His sandy-grey complexion disappeared, his wizened body, from which all blood seemed to have drained, brought forth its oils and saps as he sat in the sun each day, for he treated his body these days with a love he did not have for life itself. Like his boots, like his sword, so he treated his body, not with a selfish love, but more the love of an instrument that would be used to perform some task. (p. 150)

The "task " he has to perform is the manipulation of his final and finest moment; it is as we would expect, a consummately public one, and perfectly staged. His letters and rallies across the island have prepared him for the arrival of the Commissioner from India and his meetings with him. Kale's entrance at the airport is immaculately timed, and done with typical flair, panache, and arrogance:

An old 1936 Ford convertible surrounded by a dozen drum beaters was moving slowly into the airport. There was hardly a child left standing, they all ran towards the drummers and the car, and as they came closer, a figure could be seen sitting on the folded canvas top at the back of the car dressed in a distinguished-looking turban of bright saffron-yellow, its tail of deep-red scalloped edge hung down in front of his chest. (p. 156)

As the Commissioner emerges to a gunfire salute, Kale, no doubt in breach of protocol, and given a wide berth by the governor and officials, walks out to greet the young envoy. Kale is garlanded first by a young girl, whom he assists as she places the string of bright yellow magnolias around the neck of the Commissioner. Kale has deliberately stolen the spotlight from the young man. The two garlanded men – "the greatest soldier, leader and stickman" of the island's Indian community and the young man with a message of comfort and hope – walk along in "friendly embrace" (p. 158). Kale has upstaged everyone, as he becomes for the moment the cynosure of men, women, children, officials, and commissioner. He is given a wide official berth, perhaps because the governor, Salwan, and others know of the impending disappointment embedded in the envoy's message. Kale's much-awaited meeting with the Commissioner is fraught with an irony that he neither anticipates nor understands. His egotism, verging on hubris ("Take-um more than God... to kill this old Pathan" (p. 3)), does not permit him even to consider the possibility of disappointment and rejection. From the beginning Kale has been characterised as a man of extremes and absolutes, somewhat like the tragic hero, ripe for a fall. The trajectory of his career reveals a steady rise in his fortunes. Atop the wheel of fortune, he fails to recognise that it has been moving imperceptibly but inexorably for him.

As high as he raises his hope in the Commissioner's anticipated concurrence, so low does he fall in chagrin. It is one thing for him to be told that the past was dead and over, and that India is no longer at odds with the British; but quite another to be told that India wishes that the indentured servants would settle in Trinidad and make it their new home. These reproofs thoroughly jolt the mind and spirit of the old man, bringing him to his knees. But the coup-de-grace comes from the Commissioner's mortifying reprimand that Kale had erred in inciting Indians to rebellion and in promising repatriation. In the Commissioner's factual but stinging question, "how many people in India do you suppose know of your existence?" (p. 170), Kale experiences his worst nightmare – the callous betrayal and rejection of the indentured labourers and him, not by England this time, but by Hindustan herself! Khan's homespun simile, in its suggestions of violence and tragic irretrievability, nicely comprehends the depth of Kale's indignation and hurt: "And the old man's heart broke like a calabash that had shrivelled in the sun, its hundreds of seeds of anger of death spilling forth" (p. 170). He once caused Jamini's world to crumble; now he feels the ground move from beneath his feet. Life for this godless Pathan is suddenly blank and void, a tale told by an egotist, signifying nothing.

With all hope and comfort gone, with nothing to live for, Kale has no option but to seek death and to die with dignity. Deliberately oblivious of his waning strength and failing health, he throws caution to the wind, and becomes the stickfighter in his swansong thrust and parry. Like the ageing actor, adored by numerous fans, he reprises for the last time his role as stickfighter, for a new audience, in a different setting, in a new age. Although the young anonymous stickfighter, helped by Kale's unavoidable lapse in concentration and uncontrollable failure of vision, delivers the deathblow to the body, it is the Commissioner's frank but unfeeling words that kill the Pathan's spirit. Khan's presentation of the old Kale, from start to finish, is characterised by a telling irony, but he allows the rebel the privilege of dying as he lived: courageously and with dignity. In this paradox we sense Khan's ambivalent feelings for a grandfather he so greatly admired, and for a man whose shortcomings were all too obvious.

III

In Khan's quite different presentations of his two main characters, we sense the author's two primary intentions in *The Jumbie Bird*: one, to present the life and death of the outsized Pathan rebel; and two, more importantly, to present the benchmark pragmatism of Binti. The discrepancy between the amount of narrative time devoted to Kale and that devoted to Binti may be to some a structural flaw. Khan, however, has literary precedent. The amount of time a character spends on the narrative stage is not always commensurate with their importance or with the cruciality of their role, as is in the case of Mrs Goodenough, the furmity woman in *The Mayor of Casterbridge*. She appears a mere three times in the large narrative, but in a real sense controls the political and social fortunes of

Michael Henchard, Hardy's protagonist. Binti's time on the narrative stage is half that of Kale's, and much less than Rahim's, but her cruciality, I contend, is greater than that of either of the two men. Whether it is intentional or not, Binti emerges as the true hero(ine) of *The Jumbie Bird*, embodying a pragmatic equilibrium that is nothing short of heroic.[20] From the very outset, Binti is presented as positive, industrious, future-oriented, pragmatic, and balanced. (Her small stature is in marked contrast to her prodigious courage and strength). Binti's initial appearance is in deliberate contrast to Kale's (already discussed at length). Twenty-four pages into the narrative (Chapter 3), after she has been vilified by Kale to Jamini, Binti emerges in person, not accompanied by rapping metallic sounds, but singing the sound of her trade, "'Co-co-nut oil... Co-co-nut oil... Get your nice co-co-nut oil'" (p. 24). The staccato sounds of Kale's initial appearance are replaced by the lyricism of Binti's vending call, a lyricism that is enhanced if we hear in her song echoes of the Caribbean folk song, "Coconut Woman", popularised by Belafonte. Her facial appearance and apparel are indices of a life of hardship and devotion and her role is that of an alma mater in its literal sense of "bounteous mother", as the name "Harvest Queen" along with the emblem of a maid with an arm full of sheaves of wheat, redolent of folk regality, fertility, and reaping future rewards, suggests. Though past her prime in strength and beauty, and despite her discoloured dress, she represents the feminine principle in all its wholesomeness. *The Jumbie Bird*, then, in spite of Kale's large and lengthy appearance, celebrates the triumph of a balanced, wholesome feminism over a blinkered masculinity reminiscent of Okonkwo's in *Things Fall Apart*.[18]

Khan continues his introduction of Binti by singling her out from every other character in the novel: " ... she set her life in the balance, and made it hold its equilibrium" (p. 25). "Balance" and "equilibrium" are not mere words here; rather they are life principles for her, combining to form the basis of her heroism, clearly endorsed by the moral framework of the narrative. A victim of her husband's unflinching Pathan military masculinity, she is forced to live alone, but visits her family every Sunday, maintaining a meaningful relationship with her only son, Rahim, (taken away from her when he was just a boy (p. 9)), with her daughter-in-law, Meena, and especially with her only grandson, Jamini. Her relationship with Jamini is special because it is meant to be a counterbalance to the inordinate influence Kale has over the young boy. Kale has filled his adolescent mind with an obsession of returning to Hindustan, an obsession which Meena calls "all kind of nonsense" (p. 7), and so comprehensively has the twelve-year-old boy imbibed the teaching that it becomes a monomania. Even Kale has to chide him from time to time, reminding him that a good education is a prerequisite to returning to India. Perhaps worse than filling Jamini's mind with the obsession of returning to India is Kale's hectoring insistence that God is dead, and that Pathan needs no God (pp. 69-71). It is worth noting that in Kale's hectoring, he associates belief in God with women (p. 69). Suddenly Jamini's fragile world comes tumbling down, and the young boy experiences an emptiness and meaninglessness that severely affect all his important relationships. The world seems fuzzy and dreary as he drifts from experience to experience, evincing an apathy best evidenced in the loveless consummation of his relationship with Lakshmi amid the graves and tombs of Lapeyrouse Cemetery (p. 166). He never truly recovers from the shock of Kale's haunting revelation, until finally Binti's loving nurture fills the awful void.

Binti's pragmatism permits her to maintain her maternal relationship with Rahim, who, because of a bad business deal with Hardaker,[21] loses his business. As a result, Rahim's masculinity is compromised, and he experiences an emptiness similar to Jamini's. He loses focus, begins to spend a lot of time at the docks, and hits the bottle. His once-tender relationship (p. 9) with Meena sours, and she leaves home, and his relationship with Jamini, his only son, deteriorates abysmally. Kale's scathing reprimand (p. 138) does nothing to put things right. It is Binti who reaches out to her son in his time of need and pulls him back from the brink of total despair. After spending most of his time on the docks, Rahim returns to an empty house, sits in the darkness alone, and hears the fearful call of the jumbie bird from the calabash tree across the street.[22] The call frightens him, and in his despair assumes that it has come for him. Beside himself, emotionally exhausted, he is rescued by Binti, whose slipper-sounds mercifully replace the dreaded call of the bird, in one of the high symbolic moments of the narrative:

> "*Twee, twee twee*," the jumbie bird called for the third time, and he knew that death was only across the street... And now in the stillness

of the house, he heard the eerie *clot, clot,* [...] coming from the back
of the house. His heart pounded, [...] he listened, tense, petrified.
He heard the soft padding again *clot, clot, clot* then, 'Rahim, ay, Rahim,'
a tiny voice called, and as if out of nowhere, out of the darkness and
shadows Binti stepped into sight" (p. 123).

She is accorded an intermediary power as she intervenes between
a dispirited son and an implacable bird. This enhances her stature
and cruciality as the narrative unfolds. She defies tradition and
folklore as she, after feeding her son, and comforting him, reproves
the bird and neutralises its power: "Hey you, you black bitch,
you hiding in the calabash tree. [...] Why you ain't come an' show
your face, 'fraid of me or what" (p. 125). This may be to some
arrogance, even hubris; but it is the calculated defiance of a loving
mother doing what she must do to save her only son. Her challenge,
we are encouraged to believe, causes the bird to fly away: "[...]
no sooner had Rahim started than there was a flapping, fluttering
sound as the branches of the Calabash tree quivered, [...] and
the bird flew away[...]" (p. 126). She is the only character in the
narrative who is given the power to confront, defy, and chase away
the harbinger of death. She is the heroine with the talisman of
equilibrium and balance who counteracts the power of the bird
of evil omen.

She chastises Rahim as only a loving mother can, keeps Jamini on
the straight and narrow, respects Meena as a good wife and daughter-
in-law, and humours her estranged husband, and looks after herself.
Ignoring her husband's misogynistic ways, she never stops loving
him, and wins our admiration in a touching scene. Coming to see
Rahim one morning, and not finding him home, she, on her way out,
peeks into the old man's room and sees him doubled up and
breathing with difficulty. Instinctively, she becomes his wife once
more and resumes her wifely duties: she sweeps, tidies the room, and
disregarding his taunts, rubs him down with oil. She scolds him,
takes full control, massages him, and puts him to sleep; her instinctive sincerity reduces the outsized Pathan to a child. Her willingness
to show affection to a husband who has wronged her completely
overrides his senescent petulance. Her equilibrium does not permit
her to feel resentment or anger, nor does it permit her to seek praise
or recognition. We are never told whether Kale knows what he has
rejected, but the reader is made sensitive to the quality of care,

companionship, and affection he has sacrificed to his myopic Pathanism. Khan's intentions are clear in this scene: Binti is raised and Kale lowered in our estimation.

This scene is presented as a prolepsis of Binti's pivotal role in the death and funeral of her husband. No one knows what to do when the grave is waterlogged from recent rains. Once more Binti assumes control of the situation, and does what no man is willing to do: she offers to go down into the grave and bail out the water. Mortified by his undaunted mother, Rahim eventually descends and empties the grave. The progress of the narrative dramatises the unfolding of the hero(ine): upstaged so often by her egotistic husband, she quietly prepares herself for the defining moment. Khan is clear in his characterisation of the old woman at this juncture. Binti, no longer in her husband's shadow, reveals her true colours. Khan draws attention to one of the great symbolic moments in the novel: " […] the old woman's posture as she stood on the large mounds of red earth beside the gaping hole, the cold grey rain sky cast behind her, made her seem suddenly to possess the fire that Kale had had in him" (p. 180). Diminutive in body, with a frail voice, she assumes a gigantic stature. The old order changes, yielding place to new, and Binti standing tall emerges as the leader. With Kale's fire burning in her now, she is complete in her balance and equilibrium. All look to her and wait for her nod to start the actual burial. While others cry and mourn, she, realising the need to show "sternness" (p. 181), maintains an admirable composure, not becoming a victim of grief, though her feelings run deeper than anyone knows. As Kale so often did, she, in a quite different manner, now leads by example. As others weaken, Binti grows strong; as others falter, she moves with steady focus. The future of the family, she grasps, depends solely on her: "She seemed to possess a new strength, a new violence to take hold of Rahim, Meena, and Jamini's lives" (p. 182).

If Kale was public in every thing he did, and sought and enjoyed the limelight, Binti is self-effacing and modest. In her private, unassuming way, she achieves the impossible: she arranges a private audience with the principal of Queen's Royal College – perhaps the most prestigious secondary school in Trinidad in the 1940s – and secures a place for Jamini there. She has defied her husband's rebukes, she has defied tradition by vending coconut oil, she has defied the jumbie bird (p. 125); now she defies all odds, giving her

grandson the chance of a lifetime. Like Kale, she too believes in the
value of a good education; unlike Kale, who merely preached about
it, she makes it possible. The divisive force gone forever, she gathers
her broken family together, reuniting them under her roof on
Quarry Street, a few blocks away from their Frederick Street dwelling. She gives them a new home, a new unity, a new beginning. The
first to rise and no doubt the last to go to bed, she becomes the
matriarch, revitalising her family. Death and its attendant fears are
behind them now. Neither the grave nor death nor the jumbie bird
frightens her. She achieves her apotheosis when we grasp that her
gentle, natural, nurturing sounds have replaced the fearful call of the
jumbie bird:

> When the sun came up in the morning, the old woman was the first
> to rise. From his room behind the coal shop, the boy could hear the
> sounds to which he was becoming accustomed. *They were no longer
> bird calls* nor wind in the trees. He heard the old woman place her
> feet in her slippers, then, as if she was stretching her body, he heard
> her sigh, and then she was moving about. (184) [my italics]

Binti has replaced Kale as the leader of the family he divided; her
natural movements and sunrise sounds have replaced the nocturnal
call of the jumbie bird, and her balance, equilibrium, and complete-
ness have created a new, less ostentatious, less self-aggrandising
heroism. With Kale's death, an era passes on; with the ascendancy of
Binti, a brighter age begins. Rahim, Meena, and Jamini are benefici-
aries of the old woman's sacrificial largesse. Rahim and Meena are
reunited, Rahim has new tools, a workshop, and, best of all, fresh
hope. Jamini, at college now, will in time under the watchful tutelage
of a loving grandmother and understanding parents, reject the quon-
dam obsession of returning to Hindustan, and accept his father's
Koranic belief: "We live in Trinidad all we days, even in the Koran it
say a person should help build up the place he get he bread from"
(p. 90). Binti shares her son's view, and now has to heal the wounds
and bruises left by Kale and to detoxify the young boy's mind and
heart that for much too long the old man kept "poisoning [...] from
day to day" (p. 124).

Khan's intentions in *The Jumbie Bird* are at least twofold: one, to
fictionalise the life and death of a grandfather he admired; and two,
to present a more admirable heroism embodied in a grandmother he

loved. The Pathan military days are over, and so are the regimentation and misogyny. We cannot imagine either Rahim or Jamini as stick-fighters or rebels. These are out of place in a new dispensation of balance and equilibrium. Kale's heroism is outmoded, retrograde, and self-serving; Binti's heroism is progressive and embracing. The need for a good education, gender-balance, and belief in one's adopted country form the basis of a mode of conduct endorsed by the moral values of the novel. The extended family, each member understanding the need for sacrifice and teamwork, becomes the emblem of a nation coming together, under a leader of balance and equilibrium, to realise its true potential. In a real sense, Binti offers family and nation fresh possibilities for self-actualisation.

Notes

1. Selvon's older brother, Dennis, married Ismith's older sister, Betty, in 1941. It was at this wedding in Port of Spain that Selvon and Ismith first met. Selvon fictionalises the abortive relationship between Dennis and Betty in his first middle-class novel, *An Island Is a World* (1955).
2. Information provided by Ismith Khan in a private conversation (August 2001) with Roydon Salick.
3. It is difficult to calculate accurately how much time elapses in the narrative. At least two rainy seasons come and go. Jamini then ought to be about fifteen years old when he enters Queen's Royal College. Lakshmi is ten years old at the beginning of the narrative (p. 44), and Rahim, forty-one towards the end. (p. 119). The narrative proper begins at sunrise on Saturday morning and ends at sundown of a weekday, making *The Jumbie Bird* a fictive representation of a red-letter day in the life of the Khan family.
4. "Introduction" to *The Jumbie Bird* (Harlow: Longman, 1985), p. iv.
5. Arthur Drayton, "Ismith Khan," *Fifty Caribbean Writers*, ed. Daryl Cumber Dance (Connecticut: Greenwood), p. 251.

6. Deborah John, "An Old-Fashioned Look at Port of Spain",
    The Daily Express (August 21, 1987) 21.
7. Nothing at the end of the novel suggests that the narrative
    time extends into the 1950s, as Cobham writes (*"The Jumbie
    Bird* by Ismith Khan: A New Assessment", *The Journal of
    Commonwealth Literature*, vol. XXI, no. 1 (1986) 240). According
    to information supplied the Indian High Commission in Port
    of Spain, the first Indian commissioner to Trinidad was Mr
    Satya Charan who took office in May 1948 and left in May
    1950.
8. Both Stewart Brown ("Introduction," *The Jumbie Bird* (Harlow:
    Longman, 1985), p. iv) and Drayton ("Ismith Khan", *Fifty
    Caribbean Writers: A Bio-Bibliographical Critical Sourcebook*. Ed.
    Daryl Cumber Dance (Connecticut: Greenwood Press, 1986),
    p. 248) state that *The Jumbie Bird* is the only novel to treat in
    depth indenture and repatriation. It should be mentioned,
    however, that six years before the publication of *The Jumbie
    Bird*, Selvon in *An Island Is a World* portrayed Johnny (an
    unflattering portrait of Ismith's father, Faiez Khan, who was
    working a machine of perpetual motion) as an alcoholic jeweller,
    who champions the Back to India campaign. Johnny, his wife,
    Mary, and their grandson, Tim, along with many others, towards
    the end of the narrative, leave Trinidad by ship for India. This
    element of the novel is also the subject of Selvon's play, "Home
    Sweet India", in *Highway in the Sun and Other Plays* (Leeds:
    Peepal Tree Press, 1991). But Selvon's tone and treatment are
    less serious than Khan's. In a good-natured riposte to Selvon's
    characterisation of Faiez, Ismith in *The Jumbie Bird* names his
    insufferable lawyer, Samuel Salwan.
9. All citations are to *The Jumbie Bird* (Harlow: Longman, 1985).
10. It is customary in many Caribbean countries to cut off both
    ends of the cucumber and rub them onto the rest of the unpeeled
    vegetable until a bitter froth emerges. This, it is believed, removes
    whatever bitterness the cucumber possesses. This is one of
    the plethora of homespun tropes, allusions, and phrases, with
    which Khan colours his narrative fabric.
11. ffrench, Richard, *A Guide to the Birds of Trinidad & Tobago*
    (Pennsylvania: Harrowood Books, 1980), p. 216.
12. ffrench, *A Guide to the Birds*, p. 216.

13. In a superficial critique, Barrie Davies refers to the role of the jumbie bird as "little more than literary embroidery"(p. 284), "The Personal Sense of a Society – Minority View: Aspects of the "East Indian" Novel in the West Indies", *Studies in the Novel*, vol. 4 (Summer 1972).

14. Lloyd Brown in "The Isolated Self in West Indian Literature", *Caribbean Quarterly*, vol. 22 (nos 2-3) 1977, 54-65, writes well on the "isolato" in West Indian literature, and sees the jumbie bird "as a symbol of the triumphant possibilities of isolation" (p. 62).

15. Khan, in an interview with Daryl Cumber Dance, admits that Kale Khan is "a very highly opinionated person [...] with strong views about a great many things" (p. 123), "Conversation with Ismith Khan," *New World Adams: Conversations with Contemporary West Indian Writers*, ed. Daryl Cumber Dance (Leeds: Peepal Tree Press, 1992) 122-132.

16. Ismith Khan's words are quoted as the preamble to Lloyd Brown's entry in *Contemporary Novelists* (pp. 496-97).

17. Renu Juneja, "Representing History in *The Jumbie Bird*", WLWIE, vol. 30, no. 1 (17-28), writes well on this aspect of the novel, but does not see Binti's pragmatism as the author's alternative to the extremism of Kale and Rahim. Indeed, there is virtually nothing about Binti's role in the narrative.

18. R. M. Lacovia, "Ismith Khan and the theory of Rasa", *Black Images*, vol. 1 (1972), 23-27, argues that the coloniser uses "linguistic tricks" to deprive the colonised of homeland, property (as in Rahim's case), name, and dignity. Whether Khan knows it, according to Lacovia, he is deeply influenced by "rasa", the "primary theory in Indian aesthetics." Lacovia is factually mistaken in stating that "linguistic tricks caused Kale Kahn [sic] to leave India" (p. 23).

19. Almost certainly, Kale would have asked Jamini to get him "moorai", the Trinidadian pronunciation of *mooli*, the Hindi word for a white elongated smooth-skinned Asian radish, used mostly in pepper-sauce and salads in Trinidad. "White carrots" is Khan's deference to a foreign audience, for "moorai" is the term most frequently employed even now by those who use the pungent root. Khan's use of ethnic phrases is very inconsistent in *The Jumbie Bird*. He finds it necessary to define parenthetically

"jaldi-jaldi" (p. 4), *"roti"* (pp. 6, 110) and *"pirha"* (p. 50), yet refrains
from using either "bindi" or "tikka" for the red mark in the
centre of Binti's forehead (p. 24), or "chok(h)a" for the breakfast
of roasted tomatoes, onions, garlic, and salt that Meena prepares
for Rahim the day he goes to see Salwan (p. 110). There are
no one-word English equivalents for "bindi" and "chok(h)a".
He leaves *"chelars"* (pp. 80, 169) and *"lathi"* (pp. 78, 79, 80, 81,
82, 168, 169, 170), and *"orhani"* (pp. 171, 173) undefined as
well. Too, he leaves unexplained the non-italicised "callalloo"
(p. 83) and "cascadee" (p. 83) – not an idiolectal variant but, as
the manuscript indicates, a misprint of "cascadoo" in all editions
of the novel. "Eggplant" (p. 6) is seldom, if ever, heard in ordinary
usage in Trinidad; the West Indian term, "melongene" is often
heard, but the Hindi term, "baigan" is most widespread among
Indo-Trinidadians and others. In *A Brighter Sun*, nine years earlier,
Selvon had introduced the non-West Indian reading audience
to a variety of Bhojpuri and Hindi words.
20. Dance, *New World Adams*, p. 123.
21. Drayton, too, makes the comparison between Kale and Okonkwo
    ("Ismith Khan," *Fifty Caribbean Writers,* p. 250).
22. It is worth mentioning that the original name of Rahim's business
    partner in the manuscript of *The Jumbie Bird* is "Hanshaw".
    Khan changed it to the more evocative "Hackshaw", then settled
    for "Hardaker", a name that is more suggestive of an unfeeling
    cruelty. Ironically, there is an implied similarity of manner
    between Kale and Hardaker.
23. In island folklore there is no necessary connection between
    the jumbie bird and the calabash tree. Indeed the calabash
    tree does not figure in Trinidad folklore. According to Khan,
    there was for many decades a "sweet" (Khan's word) calabash
    tree in the north-east corner of Woodford Square (conversation
    with Roydon Salick, August 2001). The central tree of Trinidad
    (and perhaps Caribbean) folklore is the giant silk-cotton, also
    called ceiba and kapok. Khan, in *The Obeah Man*, writes,… a
    huge silk-cotton tree, "the devil tree" as it was called, because
    it was the abode of all evil spirits" (p. 18).

CHAPTER TWO

THE OBEAH MAN

I

As with Selvon, Khan took three years to publish his second novel, *The Obeah Man* (1964); and, as in Selvon's case, the second novel is quite different from the first. Selvon had read the manuscript and was excited by what he read.[1] Khan's editor at McGibbon & Kee, however, was less enthusiastic, turning down the manuscript because of the subject matter – obeah. He rejected the manuscript not on religious grounds but felt that the subject was too arcane for the average reader. Thomas Hutchinson, however, thought otherwise, and published the manuscript that needed little editing.

Khan took a huge gamble with the choice of hero for *The Obeah Man*, for the obeah man is peripheral to mainstream island culture: at best, an ambivalent figure, using the power inherent in natural objects to protect against evil and to cure bodily illnesses, at worst, perceived by many as a devil worshipper, engaging sometimes in human sacrifice. In many ways *The Obeah Man* was a much more difficult novel to write than *The Jumbie Bird*. Khan had drawn almost exclusively on his personal participation in the daily life of an urban Muslim family in *The Jumbie Bird;* for his second novel, on the contrary, he chose a subject, about which he confessed, he did not "know the first goddam thing".[2] The reader looking for insights into obeah will be disappointed.[3] Obeah is a means to a much larger end, a hazy vehicle for a focused critique of West Indian culture. Although *The Obeah Man* is not autobiographical as *The Jumbie Bird* is, Khan's intimate familiarity with Port of Spain and its environs is everywhere evident. His first-hand knowledge of the La Basse or Shanty Town, where very few outsiders venture, was a result of his frequent visits to an ironmonger who supplied the young boy's dad with scrap metal which was shipped to other countries.[4]

It appears that the subject matter and the type of the hero of Khan's second novel were established before the first novel was completed. Halfway through *The Jumbie Bird* (Chapter 7), Kale Khan, in response to Rahim's central question, "Barp, where we have to go?" (p. 90), defines colonial rule as "Obeah, a stronger Obeah than anything we have" (p. 90). Kale's metaphor is surprising because nothing in the novel prepares the reader for it; moreover obeah is in marked contrast to Kale's obsession with returning to Hindustan and with his Pathan exclusivity. Too, obeah is squarely at odds with the old man's resistance to and fear of creolisation in a land he despises. More than likely, then, Khan is establishing a point of connection and continuity between his first and second novels. Khan, through his protagonist, in effect is saying that Trinidadians need to create an indigenous, more potent obeah to neutralise and destroy colonial government. This does not materialise in *The Jumbie Bird*, although at the end with Kale dead and buried and Binti in charge of the family, we sense that a significant step in the right direction has been taken. For Kale, throughout his long adult life, had practised his own obeah in his open defiance of colonial authority. It is now Binti's turn to practice her own brand of self-effacing obeah, based on hard work, a belief in education, a reunited family working together to face fresh challenges, and equilibrium. To fashion and effect this antidote to colonialism, Khan illustrates, the nation needs the services of obeah men. *The Obeah Man*, then, defines the role of the obeah man in an island emerging from the womb of colonialism and experiencing the initial birth pangs of independence.

II

Structurally, *The Obeah Man* is on the surface a straightforward narrative: there are no shifting narrative perspectives nor a prologue nor a narrative frame of any kind as there are in *The Jumbie Bird*. Through the eyes of a third-person omniscient narrator, who closely resembles the author, Khan presents a linear, chronological narrative that covers a three-morning period – from Carnival Monday morning, when Zampi arrives by bus in Port of Spain, to Ash Wednesday morning, when Zampi and Zolda leave her hut in the La Basse for the higher ground of Diego Martin, where Zampi has been living alone for the last four years. Although there are kinetic images of moving vehicles, of travelling by bus, of walking, of dancing sensually, and of the vision of a shooting star, Khan essentially presents a slow-moving narrative, dominated by static images. Sedentary images of individuals sitting on a bus, and images of men sitting and standing at the bar, quaffing rum and conversing in one spot, indicate that Khan is interested much more in the internal development and maturation of his characters than in their physical progress. Although there is a clearly presented topography indicating that Zampi's journey to and from Diego Martin is a descent followed by an ascent, the charting of the mindscape of his hero is Khan's primary intention.[5] Zampi learns to control his anger and other negative emotions in the successful exercise of obeah; the English painter, as a result of his conversation with the obeah man, rethinks his notions of Caribbean man to be reflected in his commissioned work; and Zolda eventually acknowledges that she has done wrong, and agrees to give Zampi's way of life an honest try.

Khan's narrative is on the surface not only structurally uncomplicated but also, in a real sense, minimal: little true action takes place. Of the sixteen chapters that comprise the narrative of 148 pages (192 in the first Hutchinson edition), four (11, 12, 13, 14) are entirely set in the Scorpion Tail Club, two and a half (part of 1, part of 2, 4, 5) in the Britannia Bar, two (most of 2 part of 3, 10) on the bus that plies between Diego Martin and Port of Spain, two chapters (most of 3, 6) are set in Blue Basin on the compound of Zampi's hut, and the final two chapters are set on the La Basse, mostly inside Zolda's hut. Chapters 8 and 9 are entirely devoted to background information on Massahood and Hop and Drop respectively. These appear in the middle of the novel, and are, in their own right, splendid vignettes. They are less extra-narrative than the Prologue to *The Jumbie Bird*; however, they further retard an already slow-moving plot, a synopsis of which is an appropriate way of beginning a critique of the novel.

Zampi has become an obeah man, leaving Zolda, his woman, and Carnival behind four years ago. On Carnival Monday morning, beset by nagging doubts and rumours concerning Zolda's fidelity to him, he leaves his secluded hut in Blue Basin and descends into Port of Spain to ascertain the veracity of the rumours largely spread by Hop and Drop, the cripple. Zolda, not quite voluntarily, returns with Zampi to Blue Basin, and after violent lovemaking that awakens in her a fierce sexual desire, she feels compelled to return to the city to revel in the last hectic hours of Carnival. Zampi initially insists that he will not return to the city with her, but runs after her when he realises that the sexual desire that he awoke in her may be properly satisfied by someone else. They return by bus to the Scorpion Tail Club, where the habitués have gathered to squeeze out the last, slow drops of Carnival. Zolda puts on a special performance, specifically aimed at making Zampi jealous and hurting him, as she engages with Massahood in a blatant, sexually provocative dance. Zampi is a model of self-control as Zolda and Massahood carry on raunchily before an appreciative crowd. Zampi has the opportunity to display his obeah powers first with Massahood, then with the English painter. Defiantly, both Zolda and Massahood, lust burning in their loins, leave the club and make their way to Zolda's hut on the La Basse to consummate their newfound relationship. There, both act out a cat-and-mouse pre-coital game. Massahood becomes impatient and throws himself on Zolda, who suddenly changes her mind, and pleads with him to allow her to turn on the light. Hop and Drop quietly makes his way to the hut, and seeing Zolda's plight and hearing her frantic "no", plunges a knife into Massahood's shoulder. In a moment of mutual recognition, Massahood's rails against Hop's ingratitude, only to hear the cripple's desperate insistence, "She don't want you ... Who tell you to force she? She belong to me... to me... *me*! Me me me!"[6] An indignant Massahood picks up his stick and with a blow to the small hump on the cripple's back sends him flying among the pots and pans in the hut. Zolda attempts to protect Hop and Drop by grabbing Massahood's ankle, only to receive for her pains, a hard stomp of the stickfighter's heel on her neck. Massahood's mind reels back to childhood days and the inhuman treatment he received from Santo Pi, and feeling only "hate and resolution" (p. 130), cracks the defenceless cripple on the head, killing him instantly. Zolda, sensing her plight, and fearing for her life, runs past Massahood, and wakes up her neighbours with shouts of "Murder, Murder, Murder" (p. 131). The drowsy men and women slowly gather before Zolda's hut, and begin to taunt, revile, and stone the stickfighter, impotent with rage and hauteur. One small stone leads to another, then larger stones follow, and quickly the stickfighter slumps to the ground and dies a passive death. Zampi, unaware of all that has happened on the La Basse, leaves the Scorpion Club for Zolda's hut only to discover Massahood's corpse sprawled out on the ground, his legs wide apart, and arms flung out, and inside Zolda's hut he sees the cripple "with arms and legs drawn up tightly like an overturned bug that could not right itself" (p. 143). He finds Zolda weeping and contrite, blaming herself for leading the cripple on to his death. An understanding Zampi soothes, comforts, and forgives her. Santo Pi emerges, and in a welter of emotions, theatrically mourns his dead grandson for whom "there was no pity, no sympathy, nor love"(p. 146). Zampi and Zolda, taking only a red hurricane lantern – an apt symbol of their relationship – leave the shanty they once shared for his hut on the heights of Blue Basin that looks down on the city and the La Basse. Before he leaves the dump, Zampi swings Massahood's stick into the air and sees it land onto one of the fires on the La Basse and hears it explode, disintegrating into black ash.

III

While the literal narrative is uncomplicated, the foregoing synopsis does little justice to Khan's narrative technique in *The Obeah Man*. The *ordonnance* of literary, mythic, and symbolic patterns creates Khan's most ambitious and complex novel. Khan himself offers a confessional invitation to reader and critic in an important interview with Cumber Dance: "It's a purely symbolic novel".[7] *The Obeah Man* operates on several discrete but interrelated hermeneutical levels. Ostensibly, it is a narrative of the difficulties and rewards of becoming an obeah man: this is the one in which Khan is least interested. On another level, it is a fairly conventional love story in which the male lover goes in search of his woman about whom rumours of infidelity swirl, and, after overcoming many obstacles, brings her back home. Furthermore, like many West Indian novels,

it is a literary pastoral with the traditional antinomy at its centre
– the city is a place of soul-destroying sensuality and vice, and
the country, a resort of serenity and spiritual restoration. Mythically,
in addition, *The Obeah Man* is a Caribbeanisation of a central universal
narrative, in which the hero bests all obstacles, unmasks the beast,
and establishes a pattern of conduct and vision, worthy of emulation.
Moreover, on a level, most personal to Khan, the novel depicts
the painful condition and isolation of the artist in society. Finally,
and most significantly, *The Obeah Man* can be read as an atypical
fable of the evolution of Caribbean man represented by the four
major characters: Massahood, Zolda, Hop and Drop, and Zampi.
Khan in the above-mentioned interview establishes how central
the political reading of his novel is: what he says of Hop and Drop
is equally true of the other major characters: "… he is so
representative of the Caribbean – we are all of us always coming
up with some sort of voyage… I think they [Brathwaite and V.S.
Naipaul] are still looking for themselves, or looking for some
ancestry… I think that it is something that is very elemental to
all of us, a special significance to people who are so far removed".[8]
The following critique takes its cue from Khan, prioritising the
political reading and conflating the other hermeneutical levels.

The temporal setting provides the first obvious clue to what Khan
is doing in *The Obeah Man*. The narrative time covers a three-
morning period: it begins on Carnival Monday morning and ends on
Ash Wednesday morning. It is worth mentioning that j'ouvert, the
pre-dawn opening of Carnival, is omitted. This is not only the earliest
phase of Carnival but also the one that bests showcases the humour,
bawdiness, and lewdness of island culture. It would have provided
Khan with an ideal matrix for his symbolic critique of the nation's
definitive extravaganza. But Khan is less interested in a detailed
description of "playing mas" than Lovelace is in *The Dragon Can't
Dance* or Selvon in *Moses Migrating*. Khan with admirable control
admits the reader to a personal assessment of Carnival. If Lovelace
depicts Carnival as a celebration of the creative potential of
Trinidadians, then Khan offers a quite different perspective. The
insistent repetition of such key phrases as "savage", "wild", "ugly",
and "hungry", forms the linguistic index of Khan's deliberately
negative presentation of Carnival. His emphasis is on the spirit-
destroying aspects of the island's largest cultural festival, when taken

out of context. Indeed Carnival is Khan's symbol for the chief obstacle that prevents men and women from finding self-fulfilment. Further, Carnival is the enemy of man's inclination and urge to discover a means of spiritual cleansing and healing.

While Khan's presentation is undoubtedly lopsided, it is not totally negative. For it is not that Khan is calling for a ban on Carnival, neither is he saying that there is something unhealthy in the wanton mimicry that characterises the annual cultural celebration. Rather, he presents Carnival as insistently innate and instinctive. Zampi, after a four-year hiatus, when grabbed by a woman in a domino mask, "could almost feel his feet slip into the easy rhythm of the band" (p. 5), and was secretly pleased that a woman should accost him this way on Carnival day. And there is nothing wrong either for Zampi or for Khan in giving expression to the Carnival instinct. What is wrong is the total acquiescence in Carnival, an acquiescence that seduces one into making every day a carnival. This is counterproductive, killing its true creative spirit. This spirit best manifests itself in finding a counterpoise to Carnival. Obeah, the belief and practice of finding natural cures for ailments of body and spirit, is presented as the answer to Carnival. Carnival in *The Obeah Man* is presented as the celebration of much that is wrong with society, of what eats away at and destroys the equilibrium of society. Zampi and Khan recognise and bemoan this; Massahood, Hop and Drop, and Zolda do not. Zampi has become an obeah man showing the way and ministering to the needs of an ailing society that neither recognises nor acknowledges its sickness. When Zolda eventually agrees to eschew Carnival and seek to understand the life of obeah, we sense that Zampi renews his hope for his country. Zampi becomes a torchbearer to his fellow men, lighting up the way to a life of hope, balance, and healing.

While there is no carefully worked out pattern that interlocks the characters as we would ideally wish to see, Khan's intentions are clear in this symbolic narrative of the progress and evolution of Caribbean man. The four major characters represent different phases in the social history of the Caribbean. Although the painter is not Caribbean born, his character is carefully presented as one that impacts on the Caribbean sensibility of looking outward for solutions to an inward problem. Santo Pi, a night watchman for the Trinidad Electricity Board, is the oldest character; as one would expect he represents the earliest phase of Caribbean evolution presented in the novel. He embodies the worst characteristics of West Indian society: gratuitous violence and ingratitude, a phase defined by masculine domination. There is in this old man's life neither caring, nor sympathy, nor love. At first, when his baby grandson was left behind by his mother who went to Venezuela, Santo Pi "was glad to have someone to shout at, someone to run his errands, someone to rub his bony back when it ached with the dampness of the rainy season" (p. 58). His self-centredness prevents the impious old man for feeling any genuine affection for an orphaned blood relative. As Massahood grows, Santo Pi develops a proprietary control over and deep resentment towards the boy's natural development. An innocent, childish question about the cause of rain earns from this vicious man a slap that "choked off the boy's breath, drew blood" and that sent him "spinning like a small rag doll across the tiny little shack" (p. 58). The simile expresses the dehumanising control Santo Pi exercises over his tender grandson. This is Massahood's first vivid and memorable experience of life, galvanising the child into a life of violence. The relentless violence Santo Pi teaches him, he adopts, and he waits for the day of retribution against his grandfather. It comes, when in resentment of Massahood's vigorous development and enjoyment of food and sex, Santo Pi hacks a "great ball" of spit into the food, prepared by the grandson, and forces the contaminated food between the boy's clenched teeth. The old man lashes out with his stick. At first Massahood parries the blows, but feeling the sting of a blow to the legs, coiled up on the floor like a snake, Massahood suddenly lurches at the old man and knocks him off his feet. Instinctively, Massahood assumes the upper hand and lashes out at his grandfather's legs causing the injured man to shriek "like a small pig in the slaughterhouse" (p. 64). Again, the simile conveys the author's disdain for the old man's way of life. With ensuing cuffs and kicks, Massahood knocks the cunning out of the fallen man, and then delivers the final deserved indignity: "The boy then rolled his spit into a large ball and let it fly straight into the old man's face" (p. 64). Massahood completes his revenge by running the old man out of the La Basse before a small group of neighbours who "stood dumbly satisfied" that their anticipated day had at last arrived. Santo Pi's world comprises rejection of one's country, merciless disregard of propinquity, indignation towards the enjoyment of sexuality, and unforgiving retribution, and is characterised essentially by violence almost for the sake of violence. In Santo Pi's final appearance to mourn in vain his dead grandson, we sense Khan's ultimate criticism of early West Indian man, totally dominated by all that keeps him from moving forward. Santo Pi's life lacks the balance, equilibrium, and human sympathy that form the basis of the ideal vision of both author and obeah man.

Although Khan does not permit glimpses into Santo Pi's parentage and nurture, he clearly establishes that Massahood, the old man's solitary ward and grandchild, is a product of the night watchman's approach to life, though he adopts a less warped *modus vivendi*. The growing boy cannot escape the violence bred into him, but Khan is sympathetic to his plight by permitting him to use it less wantonly and indiscriminately. His romance with violence, the only life he knows, is acted out in the "gayelle" as he trains himself to be a champion stick fighter, who takes a voluptuous delight in what he does best.[9] He is the most successful stick fighter in the city, turning violence into a masculine art form, the objective of which is to injure or to kill one's opponent. Yet, as proficient as he is in the gayelle, he instinctively takes no chances with success: he asks Zampi to put a hex on his stick to prevent him from losing. This, combined with his virtuosity, makes him invincible and renowned throughout the city and its environs. His fame at stick fighting wins him a legion of male supporters, and his well-proportioned, muscular build makes him immensely popular with the women. This characterisation deliber-ately sets him apart from Santo Pi, giving him a vitality and an aura of sexuality the old man totally lacks. Massahood has had many women, and lives to satisfy his vast appetite for sex, food, and violence. He represents, in the political pattern, an early phase of Caribbean man's development, a phase dominated by instinct and the id, by self-preservation through violence and sexuality. Men are to be belittled and conquered, sometimes killed, in the gayelle, and women are playthings, there to be merely easy prey to his massive libido: "His women were women of the streets, each of who loved and desired like no other" (p. 126). Only Zolda poses a real sexual challenge, although he is sure that one day she will come begging. That day arrives, but turns out tragically different from what he envisioned. He dies in his attempt to force himself on her, although, to be fair to the stick fighter, he is encouraged and teased to the point of no return. Zolda, Hop and Drop (and Khan) conspire, as it were, to deny him his final libidinous pleasure. His ignominious death is Khan's criticism of Massahood's lopsided, masculine life style: "Then he fell back to the ground again, and now the angry mob moved closer in for the first time, and each man emptied his hands of the stones he had picked up from the ground upon the stick man, who must have been quite dead already" (p. 137). Massahood's nurture, life, and death form an object lesson in the progress of violence and sexuality: violence breeds violence, compulsive sexuality is self-destructive. The presentation of Massahood is in effect Khan's criticism of Caribbean man's predilection for violence and sex, even though the history of the region is one of plunder, rape, massacre, and genocide. Caribbean man must learn to deal positively with violence and sexuality, for violence is merely self-perpetuating, and loveless sexuality is invariably hoisted with its own petard. Massahood's role is characterised by an intentional irony that nullifies his achievements. Success against men and with women makes him arrogant, believing that he could beat any man and conquer any woman. After a lifetime of success, he plummets into a pathetic notoriety with the merciless killing of Hop and Drop. The most devastating irony lies in the telling ignominy of his death, reviled by all, stoned, and feebly mourned only by his feckless grandfather. Khan's critique establishes the monolithism and ultimate danger of a life merely of sex and violence: like the wounded adder it blindly turns with a fatal bite upon itself.

Unlike that of Massahood, the portrait of Zolda is largely positive, even though to a large extent she is the avatar of the spirit of Carnival, to which she is instinctively drawn as a honeybee to a nectared blossom. Zolda is at her best on the streets of Carnival, masquerading, and moving sensually to "the din of savage steel-drum rhythms" (p. 28), or in the nightclubs of the city writhing provocatively before an indulgent audience. She embodies the multi-ethnic nature of Carnival, its sensuality, its voluptuousness. In her compelling beauty and sensuality, she is a Caribbean Cleopatra, a vampiric embodiment of sensuality, living for fleshy pleasures, as she leaves hungry where most she satisfies. Too much for the stick-man, she casually entices and seduces Massahood, but at the last moment changes her mind about having sex. And she unwittingly leads the sexually helpless cripple on to believing that he owns her and that she wants only him. Away from Carnival, she mirrors Cleopatra's behaviour away from her Antony: confused, hasty, and cynical; in tune with the spirit of Carnival she is utterly desirable and irresistible. Massahood, and, to lesser extent, Hop and Drop, discover with tragic results the truth of this observation.

Only Zampi understands her ambivalent charm, its implications and effects. Appropriately, the obeah man returns with her to Blue Basin to see for himself what she is capable of. Khan is indulgent towards his heroine: her riveting beauty, carriage, and sensuality elicit the admiration of all with whom she comes into contact. While Khan denies both Massahood and Hop and Drop any opportunity of change, of discovery, of recognition of wrongdoing, he allows Zolda an aperçu at the end of the narrative. We may not be convinced by the suddenness of the change of heart, but Khan's intentions are quite clear. For his abstinence, sacrifice, and philanthropy, the obeah man has to be rewarded, and a contrite, complaisant Zolda is an appropriate reward. Whatever reservations we may have about the suitability of Zolda as a mate for Zampi are weakened by Khan's approval of her change of heart. Khan's lyricism, almost at very end, strongly suggests that what Zolda feels is the real thing, the love for Zampi that she has for so long denied: "Let love live like a lonely lost thing locked up in the heart. It will surface, shine, and see itself again as Zolda saw it now. [...] She felt that there was a gap between them that she wanted to fill in, and she waited to go with him right away with all her senses open so that she would not miss the smallest sound that the winds make when the great sea calls them back from the land" (p. 148). This, of course, marks a huge transformation from an instinctive devotee of Carnival to a conscious, willing child of Nature. Whatever ironies lurk in this convergence of hearts are unintentional.

Zolda, the only female of substance in the novel, represents in Khan's evolutionary narrative, the feminine principle, a *sine qua non* of any balanced vision and approach to life. Khan enhances her stature by making her, at least in matters of the heart, Zampi's equal. At odds initially and for most of the narrative with the obeah man, she finally comes around to admitting her guilt, and to be willing to right the wrong. Though her intellectual life is negligible, her heart is in the right place. As a result, she represents a progressive phase of Caribbean evolution, ahead of the consumptive violence of Santo Pi, the bitter self-absorption of Hop and Drop, and the unbalanced masculinity of Massahood. She represents a phase of progress and hope, future-oriented and willing to recognise past wrongs and weaknesses and to move to a new, more balanced vision, at the basis of which lie the lessons of Nature. She recognises as well the wisdom, benefit, and balance of a monogamous relationship of reciprocal love.

Quite different is the cripple. Based on Peter, a real-life character who lived on the city dump, and who, like Khan, frequented the Britannia Bar, Hop and Drop, for at least one critic, is "one of the most fascinating characters I've ever met".[10] In Chapter 9, devoted entirely to providing background information on the curious cripple, Khan's symbolic technique is evident at the outset. We learn that the cripple's face is different from others which lend themselves to story easily, and that it was an "ageless face of stone" that "did not have time stamped on it" (p. 66). Though he fills the portrait of the cripple with a wealth of physical detail, Khan is more interested in the symbolic implications of his character. There is a timeless dimension to the cripple's face and to his representation, almost as if the non-verbal facial aspects of the cripple defy the art of narrative. Khan, therefore, creates and tackles a very difficult subject. Hop and Drop is given greater intellectual credentials than anyone else in the novel, but his hubris, like Kale Khan's and Massahood's, does not go unpunished. Like Kale, Hop and Drop is a self-made man, a self-styled leader who, somewhat like the epic heroes of old, founds a community and defends its right to exist, and invites others to enhance its growth and reputation: "Man he was the first man who put up a shanty on the La Basse, and when some stupid health inspector come and bust a case in he ass and carry he up befo' the magistrate the case get dismiss. Since that time other people gone to live and make a whole town out of the place… and like he is mayor of that town" (p. 67). Such achievements would be impossible without great mental and intel-lectual preparation. To his credit Hop and Drop is able to draw heavily on "ancient books, old newspapers, magazines, some centu-ries old, which he memorised, quoted, and hoarded" (p. 68). His learning is neither superficial nor sham; he is no charlatan or confi-dence man, an important player in the drama of many cultures. He, a twisted black man from the squalor of the city dump, is able to "argue like a lawyer from London befo' the magistrate" (p. 67) and have his case dismissed. Like Tiger in *Turn Again Tiger*, Hop and Drop has learnt well the lessons of history, and has drunk deeply from the springs of knowledge; and like Tiger, his learning does not adequately prepare him for the definitive crisis.

Khan continues his mock-heroic characterisation of this unique individual by making him at once "an aristocrat" (p. 70) and a connoisseur nonpareil of rubbish: "Years of living off the refuse of other people's lives gave him an extra sense of discrimination so that his instincts led him immediately to the refuse of the rich" (p. 70). Though he lives on and off the dump, his aristocratic tendencies lead him to the best canned food, with which he stocks his larder. Caviar, for instance, is brought out on a special occasion at Zolda's shanty, and offered to the unlettered. Typically, to establish his intellectual superiority, he does not pass up the opportunity of educating them about the provenance of the food of the rich. Like many of Wordsworth's peasant heroes, Hop and Drop has "fleeting moments of grandeur when he saw himself a kind of end to all God's creations, for within his breast were tuned to a much higher pitch all the feelings of ordinary men" (p. 77). But unlike Wordsworth's peasant heroes, Hop and Drop's learning gives him a conscious superiority over his fellowmen, and leads to megalomania, albeit an innocuous one. Not content with being a "grand gourmand" (p. 70), and with legitimising habitation on the La Basse, he sees himself "as a great wedge which could crack open the British Empire," and he becomes an expert on independence for the island" (p. 71). In other words, the cripple sees himself as a political leader and freedom fighter, capable of freeing the nation from the vice of colonialism. And he is absolutely sure that the Empire will crumble (p. 71).

While all of this is positive and laudable, we discover just how limited his vision of an independent nation really is. Hop and Drop may pay lip service to the necessity of being independent, but his outlook is too negatively colonial to be truly beneficial. In this regard, he is little better than the toadyish tourist officer. He is proud of his colonial learning, but refuses to give appropriate respect to obeah, nor does he see in this indigenous art form medicines and cures for an ailing society. In spite of the cripple's "philosophising" (p. 71), Hop and Drop is part of the disease that infects a sensual, effete culture. He can predict a day of independence, but does little to effect it. So much of what he does is done out of egotism; little else other than self matters. He desires and protects Zolda, yet spreads rumours that she has been unfaithful with Massahood; he worships the stickfighter, yet drives a knife into his shoulder; and he refuses to endorse the necessity and efficacy of the vision of the native artist. He dismisses the vision of the obeah man, but openly endorses that of the English painter. In his bizarre, egotistical way, he comes to symbolise the inward drive and insistence on the need to be free. He embodies an inchoate postcolonial urgency to shake off and dismantle the systems of colonialism that seek to kill man's quest for dignity, self-worth, and self-actualisation.

The ameliorative vision of the author has compensated the cripple with class, learning, and a vision of independence for his country. This is to offset what Nature has given him: a tortured, twisted body, stumpy teeth, a humpback, and two legs of different length, from which he derives his sobriquet. Though Khan to some extent roman-ticises Hop and Drop, his realism makes the cripple unforgettable, stirring the imagination as no else does in *The Obeah Man*. For we discover that to a large extent his body is a reflective index of his mind: with all his learning, gleaned with difficulty from so many sources, he lacks basic human sympathy and sensitivity. His learning breeds a hauteur that causes him to ridicule the obeah man and his practice of obeah: "You sit on your ass, work a little obeah here, a little there, you think that you is God because you have a few pissin' tail people who come to you from the bush and make you feel great" (p. 110). Furthermore, his resentment springs from the irrational belief that because Zampi could not make him whole, that the obeah man was an agent of a wicked, brutal Nature that made him a *lusus naturae* and the laughing stock of the city. Secretly, he nurses a deep hatred for the obeah man and in his malevolence wishes to see his downfall. Though the positive aspects of his life cannot be denied, Hop and Drop, of all the characters in *The Obeah Man*, is the most cunning and devious. He harbours an inveterate hatred for God, Nature, and Man. In spite of his impressive learning, he lacks the wisdom to understand that his crippled condition is nobody's fault. And he lacks the wisdom, too, to follow Zampi's human advice "that he should learn to live with his deformity" (p. 11). As a result, he becomes an embittered, emotional cripple, living essentially for the abandon of Carnival and nurturing sexual fantasies about Zolda, who is beyond his grasp. In a novel of physically attractive men and women, he is singularly unattractive of body and heart.

Hop and Drop is, as Khan confesses, "a symbolic portrait of

someone who comes from the Caribbean".[11] But this does not get us very far, for we can say much the same of Massahood, Zolda, and Zampi. Rather, he represents the ambivalence of colonial man, having a vision of independence, yet disdaining the indigenous, mimicking the white man, and looking outwards for solutions to an internal problem. Like his real-life historical counterpart, he has read widely, can use the white man's language and laws to beat him at his own game, but cannot give appropriate respect to obeah, nor see in this indigenous art form medicines and cures for an ailing culture. With his mask of the most beautiful face and his clothes back to front, he symbolises the unenviable condition of colonial man, moving backwards and forwards simultaneously, oscillating between a drive for independence and lacking the necessary courage and vision to effect it. Ultimately, in spite of his learning and vision of independence, Hop and Drop remains a bitter, frustrated, and perfidious man. He is a traitor to this vision of independence, and in his death he is a traitor to his friendship with Massahood. Instead of giving his life to the service of his fellowman, he gives it to the stickman who perfunctorily snuffs it out. Hop and Drop's life is a shameful waste of potential because he cannot reach within nor beyond himself to embrace the comfort and balance of the other.

Quite different in body and mind from the cripple is the English painter. Though he is not native born, and does not represent a phase of the evolution of the Caribbean, he is nevertheless an essential facet of the regional gem. He represents, ironically enough, the post-independence praxis, when in spite of independence, the Caribbean refuses to look within for a proper and authentic representation of itself. The painter has been commissioned to paint a mural representing the spirit of independence. There is nothing essentially wrong in this commission except that there is no matching commission for a local artist. Khan's ameliorative vision establishes the painter as a true artist, sympathetic, sensitive, and capable of recognising that his initial convictions are inappropriate and wrong. His authenticity is evidenced when he forms an intuitive bond with Zampi, whom he recognises as a fellow artist working in a different medium. Zampi, too, recognises an intuitive nexus with the painter. Khan overtakes his contemplative foreign artist and his obeah-man protagonist, painting in words his personal version of the spirit of independence at the end of the novel when Zampi and Zolda, representing a balanced vision, leave the low-lying La Basse of violence and vacuity and head for the hills of Blue Basin, where serenity and contentment reside in and around the obeah man's sequestered hut.

Zampi is an artist and Khan's hero, who is struggling to attain an equilibrium that is the answer to the excess and dangers of Carnival. Zampi's quest is presented as an initial descent, a necessary combat against the spirit of Carnival symbolised by the beast in the Scorpion Tail Club, the coming to terms with Zolda's commitment to the festival, and the promise of a re-ascent. Zampi's four-year seclusion and abstinence may be easily underestimated, but Khan creates an appropriate social and moral context to show how heroic his commitment is. The narrative establishes that everyone is drawn to Carnival and easily sucked into its violence and sensuality. Even the deformed cripple finds his moment in Carnival and uses the national festival as a substitute for sexuality. It allows him to be the complete man that he is not; it allows him to achieve a momentary completion denied to him by Nature and society. Carnival opens her arms, embracing him with an offer of a satisfaction that once engages and embitters him.

Zampi is the only character in *The Obeah Man* who has the courage and vision to eschew the debilitating sensuality of Carnival. Like Massahood, Hop and Drop, and Zolda, Zampi for many years enjoyed what Carnival has to offer. Khan does not give us a detailed account of Zampi's past participation in Carnival, but in the experience of the other main characters, we have a good idea of what Zampi enjoyed and, more importantly, rejected. It is true that Zampi is chosen by Jimpy who convinces the reluctant young man that he is to be his successor. But Zampi has to be commended for recognising his destiny and making the first large step towards fulfilling that destiny. Zampi's progress towards the fulfilment of his destiny is the embodiment of Khan's belief outlined in all three novels: a man must find his true niche; only when he discovers it can he find fulfilment. Khan's ameliorative vision ensures that each protagonist enjoys a certain degree of fulfilment, in spite of the many ironies that beset the individual quest.

Zampi, in Khan's political patterning, represents postcolonial Caribbean man. Leaving behind the monolithism of Massahood, the facile acceptance of things embodied by Zolda, and the self-destructive bitterness of the cripple, Zampi seeks to right the wrongs of the past and heal the hurts and wounds of colonial rule. Zampi's commitment to obeah is not intuitive or visceral; it is the result of constant mental and emotional struggle. Zampi in effect commits himself to self-improvement, and by extension nation-building. His aim is not simply to achieve self control, as Ramchand first argues,[12] but to struggle to achieve a "vision which held all things together and brought them into a crystal focus that should never be explained or explored, but one should only follow the direction, feel the strength of its conviction, allow it to envelop the senses and point the way" (p. 118). This is also the artist's ideal vision of equilibrium. While it calls for moderation and self-denial, it embraces sexual pleasure: "He must know the pleasure in his groin and he must know how to prevent it from swallowing him up" (p. 119). The obeah man is not a celibate recluse; he has to enjoy the comfort of a sexual relationship with a newly committed Zolda and the balance that this bespeaks.

Zampi's progress is one of ongoing learning, not only learning more about obeah, but also learning about himself and about others. Zampi, Khan's thinking hero, realises early that the more he learns about others, the more he learns about himself. Jimpy had equipped him with the bare rudiments of obeah, leaving him to acquire by experience the necessary skill and knowledge for its successful practice. He must know the limits of his powers, and when and for whom to use his gift. For example, he puts a hex on Massahood's stick at the stick-fighter's request, but refuses to give in to Zolda's insistence on behalf of the bus driver who wants to seduce women at his will. When Zampi, in a mental welter, threatens to use obeah against Zolda, he has an unforgettable photic experience that leaves him bewildered and contrite: "No sooner had his anger burst out of him than the great star in the heavens unhinged itself and came pelting with a piercing, searing, tearing of cloth. [...] Zampi, all the energies drawn out of him, [...] began retching" (p. 18). Zampi discovers that obeah must be thought of and executed with a good mind and heart, must be done in the name of all that is good and uplifting. If it is not, then it is no different from Carnival that can so surreptitiously seduce and destroy man. This is all part and parcel of the maturing process of the obeah man, who of all the characters in the novel makes the most difficult and admirable mental and spiritual progress. The difference in response to Zolda at the start of the narrative and to her at the very end is a measure of how far Zampi has travelled emotionally. His anger, jealousy, and vindictiveness slowly give way to more positive emotions and to an equanimity that is exemplary. At the end, after having been ridiculed, defied, abused, and disgraced by an intemperate Zolda and others, Zampi finds the composure to comfort and solace a contrite Zolda, who is the indirect cause of two murders. Zampi has held his own with all who have come his way. He has Massahood on his back on the floor for the first time in the stickfighter's career; he silently bests the vitriolic cripple; he makes the painter rethink what he will reflect in his portrait; he wins the admiration of the patrons of the Scorpion Tail Club; and he wins the respect of Zolda, who agrees to live with him away from the city.

Zampi enjoys his finest symbolic moment when he unmasks the beast at the Scorpion Tail Club on Carnival Tuesday evening.[12] The "beast, the red dragons' monster", makes a dramatic entry into the lives of those gathered in the club. Screaming like some prehistoric beast in great pain, wild with agony, he is transformed into the immaterial "savage thing which hungered in the very walls of the Scorpion Tail" (p. 93). Khan's technique is unmistakable. Though he offers a physical description of the beast with his silver javelin, sharp spikes, hatchet, and tin scales covering his body, Khan is more interested in what the beast signifies. On one level, the beast represents the individual who has been totally seduced and ruined by the spirit of Carnival. So besotted he is that he cannot tell the difference between reality and mimicry. Consequently, he is paralysed without his protective dragons, "tiring from the flailing of his arms", reaching in vain to capture his "lithe and quick" dragons, without whom his masquerade is pointless. On another level, and by extension, the beast symbolises colonial man's need to be governed, entrapped, and enslaved in chains. Even Zolda, not given to much deep thinking, recognises the tragedy of the beast who, when given the freedom, cannot recognise nor much less enjoy it. He must return to servitude: "And turning to the beast with disgust, 'You is a fool. You had your chance and you didn't take it. Now look at you. You can't make a note by yourself'" (p. 95). Massahood cannot understand even the literal meaning of the scene, and unconsciously blurts out a central statement, "Tell me why that beast need them dragons. *Mister* Obeah Man" (p. 96). Zampi's quiet answer underscores a social reality rejected by both Massahood and Hop and Drop: "Everybody need people, it ain't have anybody who don't need somebody. Not even you" (p. 96). Massahood, like Zolda, not endowed with significant mental life, in his rejoinder insists on a self-sufficiency that serves only to confirm his intellectual impoverishment: "Is you who need people, boy, all I need is this," pointing to his stick, "and this," grasping a handful of his genitals [...] And I don't need nobody. Nooooobody. The whole world could haul they ass" (p. 97). Khan manipulates Massahood into making a priapic ass of himself: the stick, the man, and the genitals merge into one symbolic signifier: *homo sexualis*.

After humiliating Massahood by pinning him to the floor with his stick, Zampi approaches the beast and orders him to put down the javelin aimed at the obeah man's head. As the beast's hands lower, Zampi "place[s] both hands firmly on the mask and lifted it off gently" (p. 101), revealing a man's face covered with sweat and tears rolling down the folds of the cheeks" (p. 102). Like his counterparts in mythology, Zampi is the only one who is given the courage and authority to unmask the "ugly, grinning, vicious" beast, providing an object lesson for all. The plight of the wretched beast represents the emasculation of man by a fatal capitulation to the spirit of Carnival. Confusing an annual two-day celebration with quotidian reality, the beast is reduced to "a sobbing child" (p. 102). When Zampi orders the dragons to carry him "to catch the breeze and come back to he right senses" (p. 102), he is in effect showing the reductive effects everyday Carnival has on the body, mind, and spirit. Only when we remove the Carnival masks, and understand how Carnival can ruin man, can we return to a state of normalcy in which there are equilibrium and hope for change.[13]

Zampi has withstood temptation, unmasked the beast, displayed his powers of obeah, and shown admirable restraint and balance. Initially knocked off his feet by two masqueraders, Zampi is eventually squarely on his feet as he walks away from the La Basse with the woman he loves. This is his reward for a job well done, a reward he has indeed earned. With Massahood and Hop and Drop dead, his sexual rival and his most scathing critic are no more. His final act is significant in that he puts to rest for all time the lopsided masculinity and self-centred sensuality and violence embodied by Massahood and his magic stick: "As they left the hut the obeah man took the stick which lay at Massahood's side. He swung it over his head until it buzzed as it sliced the air, then he let it fly into one of the smouldering fires on the La Basse. Seconds later there was the sound of a small explosion from the fire that sent the stick shooting into the air, snapping, crackling, blazing . . . then it fell back into the flames, hissing like some rich and volatile substance that would consume itself to the last black ash" (p. 148). At the end of Chapter Two, on the bus to Blue Basin, Zampi has an involuntary experience when he witnesses a shooting star setting the silk cotton tree on fire; the sight overwhelms him; here, at the very end, Zampi is in total control with his deliberate act of destroying the hexed stick and all that it symbolises. This less spectacular incident is of greater significance because it symbolises Zampi's final, hard-won victory over an unthinking and reifying belligerence.

Zampi's quest represents the successful journey of Caribbean man to achieve a meaningful independence of mind, body, and spirit. Zampi, the obeah man and artist, somewhat like More Lazy in *Turn Again Tiger*, though in a quite different context, fashions an indigenous style and practice of an art form, which he uses in the service of man and nation. Zampi's obeah is presented not only as a healthy alternative to Carnival, but also the alternative to a colonial mindset that rejects any indigenous cures as it habitually looks outwards for solutions and answers. *The Obeah Man* dramatises the potential of Caribbean man to discover his true niche, to fashion his own destiny, to forge his own constitution, and to progress without an English painter and a foreign Inspector of police. In time, ideally, the sycophantic tourist officer and the bitter cripple will, instead of expending their energies in abuse and ridicule, sympathise with, and understand the ways of the obeah man, as all contribute to the uplift and maintenance of a truly independent people. Zampi, with his healing power of obeah on the one hand, and with the artist's vision, on the other, has the leverage to show his compatriots the way for a new type of personal and national governance, based on equilibrium and sensitivity.

Of all the characters in *The Obeah Man*, Zampi is the one who most often wins the sympathy and approbation of the author. The progress of the obeah man establishes a pattern of behaviour endorsed by the moral context of the novel, hence worthy of emulation. For the Caribbean to self-actualise, it must at first like all discerning readers and critics understand the difference between appearance and reality, between the masks, ugly and beautiful alike, and what lies beneath them. Zampi is not only the hero questing after mastery of obeah and a realisation of a vision of balance, but also the linchpin on which the several hermeneutical levels pivot. He is at once the lover searching for his loved one, country dweller who has left the perils of the city behind for the serenity of the country, a Caribbean version of the mythological heroes of old, native artist with an indigenous vision for himself and his nation, and postcolonial Caribbean man showing others the way of righting wrongs of the past, the benefit of blending vision with desire, and of providing a cure for what ails a moribund society. Zampi shows by example a vision of hope and endless possibility for Caribbean man.

The Obeah Man presents Khan's widest and most inclusive vision of progress for Caribbean man. He moves from the inordinate masculinity and Pathan exclusivity to the creolised vision, at the heart of which are "one of the breeds of the island that has [sic] no race, caste, no colour... having the eyes of the East Indian, the body of the Negro, the skin of the Chinese, and some of the colour of all" (p. 6), and a female who is a racially mixed as he is. It is fitting then the two racially mixed individuals move on together after the deaths of the black Hop and Drop and the Indian Massahood, one, the obeah man's worst secret enemy, the other his fiercest challenger for Zolda, the possessing of whom is a crucial factor in the extent and power of Zampi's obeah.[14] Having established sufficient proof of his authenticity as obeah man, having unmasked the beast, having shown by example the value of abstinence and self-control, having looked inward for solutions to outward problems, Zampi, though he cannot truly articulate his role as obeah man, has carried the day.[15] He has overcome a welter of negative emotions, has weathered an endless tirade of insults, vilification, and defiance, and against tremendous odds has kept his equanimity and focus. If at the beginning he could confess to the masqueraders dressed up as American soldiers, "I playing obeah man... you know a obeah man not suppose to imitate anything or anybody" (p. 28), Zampi at the end has earned the right to *be* the obeah man, who will show to a suppliant, complaisant Zolda "what the night-time like when it get dark and quiet up in Blue Basin" (p. 144), and to administer to those who make the ascent seeking his special brand of medicine. As more seek his help and advice, and more emulate him as far as they can, a healthy nation, directed by a balanced vision, will eventually emerge, vibrant and brave, ready for whatever challenges face an independent people, seeking their own appropriate style.

Notes

1. Selvon was so taken by what he read that he wrote a radio drama version of the novel. "The Magic Stick" was aired on BBC on June 19, 1971. Selvon's penchant for humour is evident in this free adaptation, in which Hop and Drop makes a stick identical to Massahood's, but, of course, without the hex. In their final fight for Zolda, the cripple with a blow to the head sends a bleeding Massahood to hospital. As the cripple calls for his prize, a disguised Zampi appears and demands the stick from the victor. He refuses, and the obeah man offers him the choice between the stick and Zolda. The cripple chooses the stick. The comic drama, in which no one dies, ends with Hop and Drop inviting everyone to "play mas" and to enjoy themselves. "The Magic Stick" is among a large number of Selvon's radio dramas that remain unpublished.

2. Dance, *New World Adams*, p. 126.

3. Khan does not for obvious reasons offer a definition of obeah in his novel. It is interesting to note the definition of obeah in Ordinance No. 6 of April 7, 1868: "The word 'Obeah' shall signify every pretended assumption of supernatural power or knowledge whatever for fraudulent or illicit purposes or for gain for the injury of any person." The punishment on conviction was imprisonment "with or without hard labour for any term not exceeding six months." See James Cummings, *Barrack-Yard Dwellers* (St. Augustine, Trinidad: UWI, School of Continuing Studies, 2004): 82-89.

4. Information in this paragraph was provided by Khan in an unpublished conversation with Roydon Salick (August 2001).

5. The Blue Basin waterfall is above the 300 ft contour in the western tip of the Northern Range. The La Basse, reclaimed land, is lower than sea-level. Khan no doubt chose Blue Basin as Zampi's abode because of its pristine natural beauty that is in marked contrast to the man-made squalor of the La Basse and the concrete jungle of the city. It is interesting to note that most of the herbalists and many well-known obeah men came from Diego Martin, the village in which the Blue Basin waterfall is located

6. All citations are from *The Obeah Man* (Toronto: TSAR, 1995).

My reading of the novel in the Introduction to the reissue is somewhat different from what is presented in this chapter, though I stand by what I wrote eleven years ago.

7. Dance, *New World Adams*, p. 132.

8. Dance, *New World Adams*, p. 132.

9. "Gayelle" is the Trinidadian word for either the enclosure in which stick-men do battle or the ring in which gamecocks fight. It has become a household world in Trinidad since the setting up of the television channel called "Gayelle".

10. Dance, *New World Adams*, p. 132.

11. Dance, *New World Adams*, p. 126.

12. Ramchand writes well but too little on *The Obeah Man* in "Obeah and the Supernatural in West Indian Literature," *Jamaica Journal*, vol. 3, no. 2 (June 1969) 52-54.

13. Lloyd Brown, in a perceptive but quite different reading of this symbolic scene, sees Zampi (and the beast, it appears) as a type of the *isolato*. "The Isolated Self in West Indian Literature," *Caribbean Quarterly*, vol. 22, nos. 2-3, 1977 (54-65) is wide-ranging, and contains excellent insights into a central aspect of Khan's first two novels.

14. Although the novel does not explicitly establish the racial origin of either Massahood or Hop and Drop, Khan clearly does in his interview with Dance (pp. 126-126). And see the paper by Jeremy Poynting, "The Construct of Order and Energy in Indo-Caribbean fiction", 2nd Conference on Indians in the Caribbean, UWI, St. Augustine, 1984, which reads the themes in the context of Trinidad's ethnic politics.

15. Lacovia, argues that Zampi's inability to articulate his role as obeah man is due to his instinctive distrust of language which, "at best provides a negative approach to reality." "Ismith Khan and the Theory of Rasa," *Black Images* 1: 3&4 (1972) : 23-27 provides meaningful insights into the difficulties language poses for several of the characters in *The Jumbie Bird* and *The Obeah Man*.

CHAPTER THREE

THE CRUCIFIXION

I

Towards the end of his interview with Cumber Dance, Khan refers
to his third novel as the work "that nobody wanted to publish".[1]
After its submission as his thesis for the Master of Arts in Creative
Writing at Johns Hopkins University in 1970, Khan sent it to two
publishers, one American, the other British. Both rejected the
manuscript: the American publisher thought the subject matter
was too "close to the Christ story"; his British counterpart stated
that it was too "slight".[2] Khan was understandably disappointed
because the novel "got some nice comments from some people"
and because it was, as he himself says, "complete" and "finished".
He did not "bother to trouble publishers and editors" again (Dance
132). Some seventeen years after the novel was written, Jeremy
Poynting in charge of Peepal Tree Press, a publishing house that
has made available so many West Indian works, learned that Khan
had a "finished" novel "sitting there", gathering dust. On perusing
the novel, he decided readily to publish *The Crucifixion*, rescuing
Khan's manuscript from certain oblivion. For, as Khan confesses,
he never "push[ed] these things too hard," and got "pissed off
real fast".[3] Khan was relieved and elated to have this work published
in his lifetime.

   The Crucifixion is Khan's last novel, and, without the author's
comments, the most difficult to assess. Khan guides the reader with
his own assessment of his protagonist: "You might say this poor devil
thinks that he has heard the voice of God one day, and God told him
that what he has to do is to go out and save people in Port of Spain

because they are sinners".[4] *The Crucifixion* is Khan's most decidedly ironic novel, as he creates a protagonist, unlike Zampi and Kale Khan, to whom he gives little sympathy and less approbation. The irony that characterises Massahoood's life and death in *The Obeah Man* to a large extent also influences the characterisation of Manko, the self-styled wayside preacher of the last novel.[5] Indeed, it is tempting to believe that in his description of the death of the stickfighter, Khan anticipates the subject matter and protagonist of his final novel: "...he was stretched out flat on the ground, his legs wide apart, his arms flung out" (p. 141). Though there is nothing remotely Christ-like or sacrificial about Massahood's life or death, there is arguably a martyrish dimension to his death by stoning and something crucifixional in the configuration of his "bruised", "bleeding" corpse.

How we are meant to interpret Manko's self-arranged crucifixion ought, of course, to be shaped by our knowledge that Khan is drawing on a well-known figure of Trinidadian folklore (and possibly real life) who also appears in *The Lonely Londoners* (1956), *Miguel Street* (1959) and *The Dragon Can't Dance* (1979). Selvon mentions Brackley as "one of them characters back home" of the same stripe as Mahal, (who walked the street pretending he was driving a car); Naipaul in the well-known short story emphasises Man-Man's eccentricity that tips over into madness; and Lovelace, in a vignette, uses Taffy as a type whose mock crucifixion appears to define the quality of life on Calvary Hill.[6] Khan does much more with the story than any of the other writers; he fleshes it out, illustrating how a particular combination of circumstances and forces – personal, social and historical – works to produce such a "poor devil" as Manko. Khan seeks to tell Manko's entire narrative – from his earliest years as an orphaned child to his final immolation as an adult – affording us telling insights into his development and evolution as social being and gospeller. In other words, he humanises the legendary urban figure, giving him feelings, discipline, weaknesses, zeal, and hubris. Although there is an underpinning irony to his folkloric narrative, Khan's presentation, detailed and serious as it is, also offers a more tragic tone in which both colonial society and Manko himself are made to share the blame for his fall. The final tableau of Manko being pelted with garbage, enduring his passion and being transformed in the witnessing policeman's vision into "Christ", creates an intriguing ambiguity that sets it apart from the other fictive versions. Are we, indeed, to wonder whether God might forgive the sinning preacher?

Khan is an urban novelist in that he uses as his setting in all three novels his birthplace and the environs in which he spent his childhood, adolescence, and early adulthood. The setting that worked well in *The Jumbie Bird* and *The Obeah Man* is reprised in his third and final novel. Frederick Street and Marine Square feature, in varying degrees of prominence, in the three novels, and the striking of the Trinity Cathedral clock marks the passage of time in all of them. Of course there are differences: in *The Jumbie Bird*, Khan privileges the activities in the Empire Bar and the Britannia Bar, in Woodford Square and in Kale's house and Binti's dwelling; in *The Obeah Man*, the slow-moving drama oscillates between the heights of Diego Martin, the Scorpion Tail Club, the streets of downtown Port of Spain and the low-lying city dump that peters out into the sea. In *The Crucifixion*, however, there is neither Blue Basin nor the La Basse; instead Khan introduces Calvary Hill, east of the city and a yard downtown on Frederick Street. Although Khan had no experience of the life of the yard as a tenant, as C.L.R. James and Alfred Mendes had, he frequented daily the yard at the back of his father's jewellery shop at 48 Frederick Street, and developed more than a passing acquaintance with several of the yard folk. Indeed, although Manko is fictional, several characters such as Miss Violet, the push cart man, and Mr. Harry are based on yard dwellers Khan knew well.[7] Khan's sketch of the yard tallies well with James's definitive description in "Triumph", although he omits what James calls "the hopelessly inadequate water-closet, unmistakable to the nose if not to the eye." Khan's description, unlike James's, establishes that the yard was walled around, effectively creating a natural theatre for the drama of life at the lowest social level. Calvary Hill, too, with its twelve bronze-depicted stations of the cross, becomes the apposite location for Manko's self-immolation on the freshly painted cross.

II

Although there are no real surprises about Khan's use of setting in *The Crucifixion*, there are things of note in his narrative technique. Much like *The Jumbie Bird* and *The Obeah Man*, the narrative of *The Crucifixion* is held together by the background and evolution of the protagonist. Khan had introduced in his first novel an extra-narrative prologue, and in his second novel he presents a multi-layered narrative that combines at least five hermeneutical levels. In *The Crucifixion*, however, Khan presents a heteroglossic narrative filtered through two discrete perspectives, offering the reader two quite distinct ways of approaching his last novel. For the reader expecting conventional linear narration *The Crucifixion*'s diffuse, centrifugal narrative of Manko's experiences in the city, intercut with the narratives of other yard dwellers, may present a challenge. Unlike James, who maintains a clear focus and chronology in *Minty Alley*, Khan's allows his narrative to oscillate between past and present, between the yard and other places in the island, challenging the reader at times to follow the narrative thread. James's narrative keeps Haynes and the yard centre-stage at all times; such events as Benoit's marriage to the nurse, which takes place at the "Church of the Rosary", are treated as if they take place in the yard. James does not take the reader into the church; instead, he allows Maisie and Miss Atwell to give two quite different versions of the wedding as they report to Haynes and Mrs. Rouse. Benoit's death at the hospital, too, is reported rather than described.

   The Crucifixion shows Khan's continuing experimentation with form and style, and is Khan's contribution to the literature of the yard, two of the most famous Trinidadian examples of which are C.L.R. James's "Triumph" (1929) and *Minty Alley* (1936). To understand Khan's contribution to the literature of the yard, it is necessary to assess James's achievement, for almost certainly Khan kept James in mind as he wrote *The Crucifixion*. Though James's subject matter in "Triumph" was new, and to many at the time of publication, shocking, the narrative technique is quite conventional. James divides his short story into two distinct sections: the first two paragraphs define and describe the yard and succinctly provides its historical background. The yard, James establishes, was the nursery of calypso, stick-fighting, the "pierrots" and other carnival practices, all of which contributed to the picturesque life of twenty-five years ago". James laments that "today that life is dead", as history and technology have transformed the life of the yard. The second section, the remainder of the narrative, illustrates the definition of the first two paragraphs. Mamitz, the heroine, and Celestine, her best friend, join forces to defeat the evil and supernatural machinations of their common enemy, Irene, who, three months before, was a good friend of both. James shows how fragile and volatile friendship in the yard can be: Mamitz accidentally knocks down the line on which Irene had hung her clothes, causing a "hot and fiery" altercation between the two friends. Irene spends her time devising ways of keeping Mamitz "in derricks", Celestine's phrase for being down and out. When Mamitz flings open the two halves of the door of her dwelling revealing "fifty dollars" spread out on the door, Irene has no answer to the taunting and general laughter of the yard. As the china bowl of rice slips from Irene's fingers and breaks into a dozen pieces, we sense the shattering triumph Mamitz, Celestine, and the yard enjoy. The events are seen through the eyes of an anonymous, third-person, narrator who does not significantly involve himself in the life of the yard. Though his sympathy for the yard is evident everywhere, except for two generalisations about women, nothing of his personality is revealed.

The narrative technique employed in "Triumph" is reprised in *Minty Alley*, a far more substantial and significant work. The third-person anonymous narrator introduces the protagonist who virtually takes over from the narrator to become the central consciousness, through whom the narrative is filtered. James carefully and consciously charts over a definitive year, the progress of his hero. In moving bourgeois Haynes into No. 2, Minty Alley, James no doubt fictionalises his own deliberate sojourn in a city yard. James must have been aware of the huge risk he was taking in creating such an exceptionally callow individual who represents an intellectually and emotionally bankrupt bourgeoisie. The narrative suggests that Haynes is unique, yet typical in his credentials. He has enjoyed the advantages of a middle-class upbringing, the benefit of seven years of high-school education, and the security of working in the only bookstore in the city. He has known the routine of bourgeois life, having lived for twenty years with a domineering mother, much too solicitous about her only child's future. Not surprisingly, he cannot think for himself, nor can this high-school graduate get simple calculations correct. Indeed, James is not convincing in using economics as the catalyst for change in this young man's life. As we shall see, James's larger intention is far more important than finding a plausible reason for moving Haynes to No. 2, Minty Alley. It is up to Ella, his mother's maid, whom he inherits, to set him straight. Significantly, it is during Ella's illness and absence from Minty Alley, that Haynes's involvement in yard life becomes most profound. After a year's experience of yard life, during which he is socialised and humanised, he moves away from the yard into rooms secured by Ella, no doubt, to resume his bourgeois life.

The triumph of *Minty Alley* is the cogent illustration of the transforming and redemptive possibilities of yard life. James skilfully manipulates his narrative to convince us of Haynes's gradual, almost imperceptible involvement in the life of the yard. One by one, the yard dwellers visit his room: a screaming Sonny, escaping his mother's savage whipping, is the first to visit Haynes, who is horrified at the nurse's brutality. As the blows and screams persist when the child is forced to leave his room, he throws himself on his pillow and cries, perhaps for the first time in his adult life. This incident elicits emotions and sentiments that have lain dormant in Haynes; this is the first step of a humanising journey. The second visitor is Sonny's mother, who comes to explain her treatment of her "only child", and to tend to Haynes's injured foot, which according to her, has been "festering" (p. 48), and has caused a fever. The nurse toys with Haynes's emotions, manipulating him into lending her two dollars, and urging him to board with Mrs. Rouse to help her out. Miss Atwell visits next, and she and Ella both attempt to convince Haynes that the nurse is "a dangerous woman" (p. 49), who has been deliberately applying the wrong medication. When Miss Atwell whispers to him that the nurse and Mrs. Rouse are trying to put him against Ella and get him "into their clutches" (p. 53), the bourgeois sensibility instinctively rises in defence of his mother's maid: "Haynes decided that he would give a very prompt and definite no to any further attempts of the nurse and Mrs. Rouse to substitute themselves for Ella ..." (p. 53).

News of the nurse's imminent eviction from No.2, Minty Alley and the expectation of yard drama transform him into a voyeur: "He glued his eyes to the peephole which he had enlarged and arranged (and camouflaged) so as to command a wide and comprehensive view of the whole yard" (p. 54). Yard life has begun to fascinate and intrigue him to such an extent that he goes to unexpected extremes to ensure that he misses none of it. This eviction is not only a turning point in the life of the yard but also in the progress of Haynes. For the first time in his stay at No.2, Minty Alley, "every separate member of the household paid him a visit that night" (p. 58). He has become in a real sense the centre of yard life. Finally, Maisie, Haynes's foil, in her typically iconoclastic way, enters through the window for her first of many visits that transform the young man. She is much more than a "firebrand", to use Ramchand's word;[8] she is a mischief-maker, a liar, a thief, an extortionist, a blackmailer, and, worst of all, a racist. She does not despise Philomen because she is a faithful and indefatigable servant to Mrs. Rouse, but because she is a "coolie". James, however, stoutly defends Philomen and Indians (pp. 85, 95, 114, 194). So protective is James towards Philomen that he gives her the last laugh: "Philomen […] grows fatter than ever and is happy because she is high in the good graces of Sugdeo. She and Haynes are good friends…" (p. 243).

Of all the characters of No.2, Minty Alley, none affects Haynes as powerfully and profoundly as Maisie. She is the human agent of Haynes's transformation. Her seduction is gradual and well orches-trated. At first she keeps her distance, then allows him to see that she "was a damned pretty girl, and would be very nice to sleep with" (p. 78). She gently leads him on, teaching him how to laugh: "… he started to chuckle too. Maisie's laugh was infectious, and of late she was always telling things that set him chuckling" (p. 115). She introduces him to romance, invites him to have sex, and remains the soul of discretion. She is his first friend, and teaches him the value of friendship (p. 194). Though three years his junior, she is older in experience and quickly realises that Haynes is being taken advantage of at work. She advises him to ask for a raise, and nags him until he does, giving him the confidence to confess about his boss, "I am going to manage him in future" (p. 172). When the final showdown between Mrs. Rouse and Maisie occurs, and Maisie leaves, Haynes realises, to his credit, that his life at No.2, Minty Alley has come to an end because his transforming agent is no longer there.

Minty Alley comprises two interweaving narratives: that of the relationship between Haynes and Maisie, and that of the final year of an eighteen-year-old relationship between McCarthy Benoit and

Alice Rouse, whom Benoit has heartlessly taken advantage of, even to
the extent of behaving as if he was a pimp. Mrs. Rouse, on the other
hand, forgives him for his affair with the nurse in her own house;
resigns herself to the hurt his public wedding causes; takes him back
when the nurse's affection waxes cold; visits him in the hospital; and
finally brings his body to be "buried from home" (p. 242). Their
entwined histories dominate life at No.2, Minty Alley to such extent
that with the passing of Benoit and the relocation of Mrs. Rouse, life
in the yard comes to an end. Indeed, it is soon after transformed into
a bourgeois dwelling, complete with the sounds of a piano being
played.

Until that point, the narrative has established that the life of the
yard is in many ways superior to bourgeois life. Behind the "squalid
adversity", there is a life of romance, passion, intrigue, colour, and
love. James establishes the worth of the working class and celebrates
its authenticity and its ability to transform the most inert bourgeois.

The Crucifixion, likewise, comprises two narratives, though they
are more clearly demarcated than those in *Minty Alley*. In *Minty Alley*
the narratives are seamless as James opts for a continuous narrative
filtered through a bourgeois sensibility that gradually grows in
understanding of yard life. In *The Crucifixion*, however, Khan employs two discrete narrative voices, each doing something different.
The first voice is a conventional voice that employs for the most part
standard English. The perspective of this voice is that of *spectator ab
extra*, of one from the outside looking in. This is the outsider voice.
The other is a far more interesting voice that uses Trinidadian Creole
in what is essentially an oral performance. This insider voice sounds
very much like the voice of a yard dweller. Unlike *Minty Alley*, *The
Crucifixion* is a hybridised narrative, resembling somewhat Selvon's
The Housing Lark, as it juxtaposes a scribal narrative with an oral
delivery. The outsider voice or the scribal perspective presents the
narrative of Manko, the self-styled wayside preacher, who dominates
each of the eight sections. It charts the progress of the preacher from
his defining moment at fourteen, through his few years in the city, to
his final mock crucifixion on Calvary Hill. This is a conventional
narrative that seeks to understand what drives Manko to commit
himself to such an unpopular calling. Consequently, Khan furnishes
us with background material, emphasises Manko's preparation and
credentials, and establishes that Manko in all that he does is fulfilling

his destiny. Much of this scribal narrative takes place outside the yard in which Manko has taken up residence: in the bars, in the Court House, in the street outside the Chinese parlour, and on Calvary Hill. Only the sixth section is set in the yard, when Manko, with help from yard dwellers, administers the public tests to establish guilt or innocence. This narrative, in normal font, is Khan's primary narrative.

The insider narrative, ironically, is secondary to the central narrative of Manko's development; it is italicised. Compared to James's narrative, Khan's is diffuse. James maintains strict control over his material: life at No.2, Minty Alley is his primary focus, and it is the centripetal topos of the novel. As noted above, such important events as Benoit's wedding and his death, both of which occur outside of the yard, are brought by the tellers of these events into the yard. Khan, however, is more liberal and wider in focus in his insider narrative, which comprises seven sections, only the first of which is devoted to Manko. The remaining six focus on several characters, some of whom have only a tangential relationship with Manko: Miss Violet (2), Thinny Boney (3), Miss B and Tommy (4), the police (5), Miss Violet and the Cripple (6), and Tall Boy, the Chinese proprietor (7). Their stories, particularly sections three and five, are sometimes only tenuously connected to the linear outsider narrative of Manko's "progress". Each section is in effect a short story that could almost stand on its own, and in linear narrative terms, though not in theme, they are independent of each other. Indeed the third section, the pushcart man's story of his conflicted childhood, minus the first six paragraphs was published some twenty-two years before as "The Red Ball". The outsider narrative, on the contrary, is a chronologically and consecutively unfolding account of Manko's ambivalent progress; no one of the eight episodes can stand on its own. Reading *The Crucifixion* as if it was a single, seamless conventional narrative presents real difficulties in continuity; from this perspective much seems arbitrary, even slipshod; reading it, however, as two separate narratives, divergent and yet convergent, yields better results: one is able with ease to follow the sustained, sequential narrative of Manko fulfilling his destiny; and one grasps that the insider narratives of the lives of the yard dwellers comment ironically on the illusory certainties of Manko's mission. The reader is invited to see the real complexity and different linear scale of the experience that has brought each of the yard-dwellers to their particular point of crisis, and to see that

Manko, with his absolute confidence in his role as God's judge on earth, is wholly unable to appreciate their needs or what is in their hearts.

To understand the difference between the two narrative voices a critical comparison of the initial sections is necessary. Indeed, this is the only comparison possible since these are the only two sections in which Manko is dominant. The outsider voice begins with a statement that seems to establish a psychological truth, but in its absoluteness hints at irony: "There was nothing that Manko wished for that did not come his way" (p. 7). In fact this initial section to a large extent deals with Manko's internal life, that of his mind, heart, and spirit; the narrative of Manko's progress is essentially the development of the preacher's mind and emotions. Although he always sought after something to make his "body and being complete" (p. 7), he spends all his time preparing his mind, emotions, heart, and spirit in the service of the Lord. His body and bodily needs are taken for granted; consequently, there is little or no need for food and sex, though he is a habitual drinker. The opening statement of the outsider's voice compares interestingly with that of *Minty Alley*: "Haynes concluded his calculations and decided that he could not continue to live in the whole house." Both are straightforward, unconvoluted sentences, free from ambiguity, but *Minty Alley*'s is about a rational pragmatic choice; *The Crucifixion*'s seems equally straightforward, but hints at hubris.

The opening sentence of the insider voice is, however, markedly different: "*Now, it have a way they teach we how to write a book in school and it have a way we have to write a book about a certain kinda people who come from a certain kinda place*" (p. 13). Its rhythm and tone are new; the iambic cadences of standard English give way to the more arbitrary intonations of Trinidad Creole. The casual, conversational "*Now*", the non-standard, insistent "*it have*", the non-standard grammar of "*teach we*", and the musical repetition of "*a certain kinda*" sweetly captures the intimacy and flavour of the vernacular. Far from being the bald, declarative sentence of the outsider's voice, this insider's sentence is weighty and purposeful, offering rationalisation, insight, and pride in doing something right. It defends and rationalises the use of the Creole in the service of authenticity; it draws attention to its slight postmodernist lisp, and it establishes that it recognises the difference between the conventional ("*it have a way they teach we to write a book*") and the necessary ("*it have a way we have to write a book*"). It further establishes that the subject matter ought to determine the narrative technique. No voice other than the insider voice, then, is qualified or appropriate. Unlike James, Khan explains his narrative technique and the reason for it, intimating to the reader that he is to expect and engage in a novel reading experience.

The opening sections are quite different in content as well. The first section of the outsider narrative presents an idealised picture of a young country boy who, everybody believes, is "a messenger of the Lord sent to dwell among them" (p. 8). Manko is awakened one morning by a small green parrot, which immediately becomes his only friend. God moves in mysterious ways, and Manko believes that the parrot's "Wake up! Wake up!" is in reality a wake-up call from God. God had used doves, sparrows, and ravens in biblical times, and there is no reason why He would not now use an indigenous, secular bird. He teaches the parrot to talk with "the deep rich intonations of his voice" (p. 9), a feat that certainly strains our credulity. (If this is Manko's perception rather than the narrator's, then it may be the onset of the young man's self-deception). At fourteen, Manko experiences a defining moment when he first meets the preacher, the most impressive man he has ever met. Manko commits himself to reading and pays to receive knowledge from the philosopher, who hangs around the rumshop. He attends the preacher's meetings faithfully and sees how the preacher's words and gestures affect the crowd. As the preacher picks up the coins on the banana leaf, Manko believes he has caught the older man. He decides that when his time comes, he will be a much better preacher, able to see "behind the veils that men cover themselves with" (p. 12). He consciously and meticulously prepares himself for serving the Lord who has provided the necessary signs. However, as suggested above, Manko never has the humility or imagination to penetrate the veils, because for him such insights are about power over others, not empathy.

The insider narrative tells a different story; furthermore, the parrot, the philosopher, and the older preacher are completely omitted. The insider voice is far more sympathetic and sensitive to Manko's situation. He is a fellow Trinidadian who knows the culture well; he knows that Manko "went up to fourth standard" (p. 14), then went to the orphanage. The mention of the orphanage is the cue for a three-paragraph digression, so characteristic of informal West Indian storytelling. He informs us too that Manko worked in the office of a doctor, who promised to teach him *"to be a doctor"* (p. 16). The doctor who strings Manko along appears to represent the colonial masters and their empty promises; this is the insider voice, a reminder to his audience of the treachery of the colonialism. The insider voice establishes his grasp of the lamentable state of island culture: *"Now, is very hard to find a job in Trinidad. Is very hard even if you find a job and keep the dam job. Is very hard if you find the job and keep the job, to understand why the ass you take the job in the first place"* (p. 16). Whatever frustrations the islanders experience are, according to the insider voice, self imposed, *"But Trinidadians born chupid, so that is the way they tink"* (p. 16). It asks the pivotal questions in a peculiarly Trinidad Creole accent, *"What the ass to do wid meself?"* (p.17). This is the question that impels the novel to its conclusion and drives Manko to his self-styled crucifixion. Whereas the outsider voice asks for reasons for the disappearance of Manko's family, the insider voice simply accepts it as part of island life. Where the outsider voice establishes Manko's obsession with becoming a preacher, the insider voice understands that it is the only thing he can do. The insider voice closes the first section with a series of ontological questions: *"Why the hell a man can't come into this world and have a good time and go out of it? Why he have to ask heself all the time what to do wid heself?"* (p.17). Unlike the outsider voice, the insider voice deliberately creates a telling cultural picture, unafraid of criticising a culture that because of the lack of opportunities has marginalised the working class.

Perhaps the central difficulty the reader encounters with *The Crucifixion* is gauging how he should take Khan's characterisation of Manko. The first sections of both voices establish both the sincerity of the young man's desire to become a preacher and his belief that he could be a better preacher than the old man. At the same time, though, Khan leaves little doubt about the nature of the young man's preparation to be a preacher; it is essentially theatrical, that of an actor preparing for a definitive performance. Consciously, Manko improves on the old preacher's appearance: he grows his beard and hair, dons a white robe, lets his fingernails grow long, and hears God's voice telling him to wear sandals. Convinced that God wanted him "to be an even more diligent servant" (p. 19) than the old preacher, Manko is meticulous and studied in his ongoing preparation:

And so during the week he prepared himself, his body and soul. He read aloud from the great Bible, and chose a section from the book of Job which he rehearsed in front of his shaving mirror. He lifted his eyebrows, he lowered them, he leaned far backwards, then pitched forward. He held his hands up in the air, he held them to his temples until he had all the gestures he needed to fit each line of the psalm he would hurl at the people in the junction. (p. 19)

His preparation reaps rich rewards, for his preaching, worshippers are convinced, truly reveals the power and presence of God. His sincerity is such that the onlookers quickly are involved as they pick up "the rhythm and intonation of his voice" (p. 20), and repeat their prayers after him. They ask for forgiveness and willingly drop their offerings on his cloth. As Manko experiences a spiritual high, the old preacher reappears as a further test of Manko's commitment. The old preacher, driven by anger and resentment, forces his way through the worshippers and swings a "crashing blow on Manko's head, with the public accusation, 'You nasty little thief... you gone and thief my spot" (p. 21). The crowd rallies behind Manko and reciprocates with their own condemnation: "The old man is a crook" (p. 21). Manko's equanimity, the parrot's repeating of Manko's plea to God, "Speak, Speak", Manko's soulful whispering of Psalm 23, the old preacher's psalm, the congregation's response, all coalesce to drive the old preacher to further violence, bringing down a crashing blow with the back of his hand on Manko's face (p. 24). Manko is accused, humiliated, and beaten; in his unprecedented plight, he compares himself with Christ: "He thought of how the Lord was beaten and humiliated before his crucifixion, and Manko felt his pain. His face duplicated the suffering he imagined Christ had suffered... (p. 22). We may not doubt the sincerity of Manko's feelings, but cannot help but note the fatal self-aggrandisement.

This is Manko's first crucifixion in the novel; this is essentially an emotional crucifixion, though he is hit hard twice and the old preacher sits on his chest throughout the accusations and blows. Manko is unable to defend himself; John-John, however, rises to his defence by first accusing the old preacher of being a "crook" (p. 25) and then by hitting him on the neck. The preacher disappears into the canefields and from the narrative. This is Manko's first real test and, with the help of others, he wins his first victory. He therefore establishes his readiness for his necessary move to the city where "all the rumshops, all the rogues and rascals" are to be found. Zampi, in *The Obeah Man*, finds it necessary to move away from the city to Blue Basin, where he finds peace, security, and meaning; Manko is drawn to the city to prove himself. Both Zampi and Manko see the city as a place of sin; unlike the obeah man, the preacher is buoyant with excitement as the bus nears Marine Square: "...he was filled with joy, a mild gurgling and churning spread from his stomach. He felt as though he was carrying out a plan which was ordained, something which had been planned over a number of years and now going into being with precision" (p. 26). Not even Tiger in *A Brighter Sun* nor Shellie in *Green Days by the River* feels such excitement on his first trip to Port of Spain. Ironically, Manko's level of excitement is an index of the profundity of his self-deception in the city.

Manko, who even when young longed for something "to make his body and being complete" (p. 7), is seduced in the city away from the desired equilibrium. He who knew he could become a better preacher than the old man becomes the victim of a massive self-deception that shatters his soul. Having enjoyed a real victory over the old preacher, and having won the respect and admiration of the congregation, Manko is convinced "... as he never was before that he was called into the service of God" (p. 25). Reasoning that he is fulfilling his destiny, he leaves his sugar-cane town for a room in a yard in the heart of the city. His contact with the workers on Calvary Hill and with the yard dwellers, especially Miss Violet, transforms Manko from a young preacher bursting with the expectation of success into a an individual prone to righteous anger, indignation, and violence. His initial frigid reception in the yard from Miss Violet is a prolepsis of what awaits him in the city to which he has a fatal attraction. Miss Violet's vast knowledge of men instinctively picks him out as a charlatan: "I don't know nothing bout Bible and sermon and sin, but I know **men**. It get so I could smell one from the other and when I smell a rotten one, I know him" (p. 48). She, the prostitute, becomes the perfect foil for Manko, the preacher. She reviles him, accuses him of being a woman-iser and a peeping Tom, and, with the help of Constable James, one of her many lovers, brings him before the city magistrate. Khan deliber-ately leaves the veracity of the accusation inconclusive even though Manko wins his case. So compelling is Miss Violet's accusation that Manko doubts himself, "... he found that somewhere in the darkness of his memory he knew what she looked like undressed" (p. 48).

Manko's trial is an opportunity for Khan to take a critical look at the judiciary of the island and to introduce the theme of justice as an ethical value; the preacher and the justice system are both on trial. Khan draws attention to the all-too-easy venality of the police, whose credibility is further compromised by the frivolity of many of their charges. The courtroom, the fortress of justice, is turned by both police and spectators into a vulgar theatre of amusement: "It was like going to the motion pictures, more amusing at times, as many of the cases were forced from the pathetic to the ridiculous, and sometime the prosecutor as well as the magistrate went out their way to ridicule the accused" (p. 61). Though young and deficient in understanding and human feeling, the magistrate dispenses justice. He dismisses the absurd case against the one-legged man on a crutch, chastises and warns the laughing spectators, upbraids Constable James for man-handling Manko, publicly insults Miss Violet, calling her "ill-man-nered", "ill-bred", and "an abomination" (p. 72), and rules in favour of Manko. He fines both Miss Violet and Constable James five pounds each for wasting the court's time, and twenty shillings for inconveniencing the preacher. Yet, as fair as his judgment is and as admirable as his commitment to and defence of the judicial system are, he is far for being the ideal magistrate. Prone to "temper" (p. 69), he resents the preacher's passivity, and is tempted to "let Manko suffer" simply because the accused rests his plea on his faith in God. Khan details the young magistrate's reasoning to highlight its obvious flaws (p. 70). His elation over his reasoning and his fresh sense of the fascination of justice is Khan's open criticism of those with power and authority who make decisions that affect the lives of others.

Miss Violet and the magistrate differ markedly in their assessment of the preacher. She instinctively knows that Manko is a fraud; he reasons that he is not. This ambivalence not only characterises Khan's deliberate presentation of Manko, but also reflects the reader's dilemma. Manko's initial attraction to the old preacher and his preparation suggest a decidedly theatrical fascination with his chosen vocation. He is also ironically drawn to the yard, another theatre of human behaviour. There is nothing inherently wrong with this; he convinces others and himself that he is a true messenger of the Lord. But Manko errs in becoming not a preacher but a "hot" gospeller, who allows his zeal to upset his equilibrium. Nothing suggests that

Manko is insincere in the pursuit of his destiny; yet there is an inkling of an overzealousness in the initial stages as he waits to see the signs and hear the call. Khan gives him a hubris that recalls that of Kale Khan in *The Jumbie Bird* and of Massahood and the cripple in *The Obeah Man*. Whereas they insist that they do not need God and that God does not exist, Manko quickly corrects himself: "He had read in the Bible about times when God's voice had come like a mighty roar of thunder out of the skies, and he came close to threatening God at times to speak to him, but again he was filled with the fear of the consequences" (p. 18). God could very well be displeased and be violent with him.

Whereas violence from God is, we must assume, invariably right and properly directed, violence in and from man must be reined in and sublimated. Kale Khan becomes violent in the assertion of his dignity as a human being as he leads his fellow Indians against the police; Zampi is violent in the protection of his obeah. Manko, the old preacher, and Constable James are all too easily moved to violence. Khan abhors violence and shows in each novel that violence breeds violence, that in most cases it is counterproductive, and that it is a primary ill of Caribbean society. It is represented throughout his fiction, but never sanctioned, except when it leads to some personal, communal, or national good. The city is a place of violence, and so is the yard. The city yard brings out the worst in Manko. Always solitary, after a short time in the yard, he loses his temper. Unlike the magistrate, Manko gives in to his need for revenge at the workmen's irreverence at Calvary Hill: "Manko was still angry, and he wished to complain, to punish; he desired revenge for a hurt that remained unclear in his mind . [...] The thought was a frightening one, but the strength and power it gave Manko to seek God's revenge was exciting" (p. 37). After complaining to the foreman and berating the workmen, Manko demands that they repent. The natural question of the workman, "How you mean repent?" (p. 38), unleashes the violence in Manko. He grasped the man by the neck of his collar, dragged him close to the bust, and forced him down on his knees. After the trial which establishes his innocence, he is filled with "disgust" and "hate" and wonders why the devil in man had "to be routed [sic] out of them with force and violence?" (p. 73).

III

The foregoing analyses show the similarities and differences between the fictional worlds of James and Khan. The differences, to be sure, are more crucial than the similarities. Both depict the fundamentals of yard life: sex, often bartered, brutal violence, a sense of frustration with one's lot, and the development of strategies to cope with the wretchedness of life. Yet James's world is quite different from Khan's, and the difference is due to the author's intentions. James presents a yard life with redeeming possibilities: Philomen is content with her relationship with Sugdeo; Mrs. Rouse is sure she will manage away from Minty Alley; Maisie and the nurse are on their way to America; and Haynes, back with Ella, has meaningfully internalised his year in the yard. James's depiction of yard life seems romanticised when compared to Khan's, for most of his dwellers move on to better things. Khan, on the other hand, presents yard life as a theatre of squalor, of gratuitous violence, of theft, of jealousy, of clandestine sexuality, and of wilful testing. Indeed, where James presents the year in the yard as a necessary stage in the maturation of Haynes, Khan depicts yard life as a test for Manko, a test that he fails. Manko is conned into a wrongful accusation of Miss Violet and into a massive self-deception by his overzealousness, which, in turn, generates the same judgemental spirit among the yard dwellers. Hankering after truth and the justification of faith in the Lord, they become judge and jury, sentencing an innocent Miss Violet to ignominious public condemnation and ousting her from the yard. The bleakness of Khan's treatment is perhaps best seen in Miss Violet's and Manko's reaction to the truth: she is forced into the arms of a decrepit cripple who offers her sex and temporary shelter, and a chagrined Manko pleads to be crucified on Calvary Hill. The yard of *The Crucifixion* has no exits as that of *Minty Alley* has. No.2, Minty Alley is transformed by time and progress into a bourgeois dwelling; this is James's reminder that when closely examined, with sympathy, the yard is closer to middle-class living than we choose to admit. Time, James suggests, is the ultimate social equaliser. Khan's yard, however, experiences no such change, as time appears to stand still. The yard remains in squalor, much poorer without Miss

Violet and Manko, its two main players. Without Miss Violet to befriend and compensate the children for the punishments they suffer, and without Manko, even as an ambivalent role model, Khan's yard is without help and hope.

The difference between the fictional worlds of *Minty Alley* and *The Crucifixion*, though, is a reflection of a historical reality. A look at James Cummings's *Barrack-Yard Dwellers* (2004) provides a corrective to the perception than James and Khan are at odds with each other.[9] Cummings establishes that there were different kinds of yards in the city and different classes of dwellers. He states that the majority of yard dwellers were Afro-Trinidadians, with a sprinkling of Afro-Caribbean individuals, especially from Barbados. There were, too, "coolie yards" and "Indian yards," dominated by Indo-Trinidadians, who had moved from the country and the sugar-cane experience; these folk popularised Indian cuisine among all yard dwellers. In addition, there were Venezuelans, Portuguese, and even local "fallen whites", who were given token jobs to avoid being employed among the labouring classes. There were "financially successful barrack-yard dwellers" whose dress, furniture and lives reflected bourgeois aspirations, and there were the most indigent who had to endure the drabbest of dwellings because they could not afford wallpaper or paint. Their dwellings were a metonymy for their wretched lives.

James's yard dwellers in *Minty Alley*, compared to Khan's, are the financially successful ones, whose living touched the fringes of the middle-class world. Their attire, complete with fashionable hats, their manner, their sitting down to a Boxing Day lunch, with "everybody officially dressed" (p. 149), sharing a quart of champagne, a pint of whisky and vermouth, and the making of speeches indicate their closeness to the higher social strata. In addition, at least two yard dwellers, Haynes and Miss Atwell, are avid readers, and associated with the world of books. Somewhat lower socially are the yard folk of "Triumph", who settle for stout and rum, because they cannot afford champagne, vermouth, or whisky. At the very bottom of the social hierarchy are Khan's yard folk, eking out a most precarious existence as they wrestle ceaselessly with myriad social evils. While Celestine in "Triumph" is able, because of Nicholas's generosity, to spread out fifty dollars on the two halves of the door, the pushcart man in *The Crucifixion* secures, with the utmost thrift, life-savings of six shillings. Unlike the yard of *Minty Alley*, near Victoria Square, the yard of *The Crucifixion* is on Frederick Street, a downtown yard whose environment was "humiliating and definitely geared to social domination and social control".[10] These yards contained crude toilet facilities that were embarrassing and unhealthy, offering no privacy to their users. Families found it impossible to achieve self-confidence and self-respect, and the yards were "always littered with rubble and rubbish". Cummings's sentence accurately adumbrates the quality of yard existence in *The Crucifixion*: "The landlords and their agents collected their rents and left the dwellers to reproduce themselves in the mire of what was considered to be a perpetual underclass".[11]

James's fictional world in *Minty Alley* admits the possibilities of positive change and upward mobility, however slight; Khan's world is yard life at its most wretched. The vitality of Maisie, the exemplary service of Philomen, the long-suffering commitment of Mrs. Rouse, and the progressive outlook of Miss Atwell light up the yard life of No.2, Minty Alley, showing the way out and forward. In *The Crucifixion* there is only "the short glow of morning light" (p. 29) coming from behind the hills; there is no one or anything to brighten the drab, bleak prospects of the yard dwellers. Even the preacher is forced into a huge wrongdoing and self-deception, so much so that God seems absent from the yard. James's yard folk at their leisure smile, eat, move lithely about on a wide, companionable stage; Khan's yard dwellers, on the contrary, are hemmed in by a wall of squalor and poverty, forced to act out the scenes of an abysmal social tragedy.

Notes

1. Dance, *New World Adams*, p. 132.
2. This information was provided by Ismith Khan in an unpublished conversation with Roydon Salick (August 2001).
3. Dance, *New World Adams*, p. 132.
4. Dance, *New World Adams*, p. 132.

5. It is interesting to note that the name Manko is not commonly heard in Trinidad, though it is also the name of the male protagonist of Selvon's "A Drink of Water" (1968), and of the obeah man in *Those Who Eat the Cascadura* (1972*)*.

6. See John Thieme, *The Web of Allusion* (Aarhus, Dangeroo Press, 1987), p. 205; and Dance, *New World Adams*, pp. 151-152.

7. This information was provided by Ismith Khan in an unpublished conversation with Roydon Salick (August 2001).

8. Kenneth Ramchand, "Introduction", *Minty Alley* (London: New Beacon Books, 1971), p. 14.

9. James Cummings's book, *Barrack-Yard Dwellers* (St. Augustine: UWI Continuing Studies, 2004), is highly recommended.

10. Cummings, *Barrack-Yard Dwellers,* p. 27.

11. Cummings, *Barrack-Yard Dwellers,* p. 27.

CHAPTER FOUR

A DAY IN THE COUNTRY & OTHER STORIES

Khan's only collection of short stories, *A Day in the Country & Other Stories* (1994), was published by Peepal Tree Press, which seven years before had published his third and final novel, *The Crucifixion*. Jeremy Poynting agreed to publish the collection, giving Khan the privilege of choosing the short stories.[1] Khan in his lifetime wrote twenty-four short stories, seven of which were published between 1955 and 1980. Of these, Khan chose only three for the collection, "The Red Ball", Shadows Move in the Britannia Bar", and "A Day in the Country"; to these he added six previously unpublished stories. Khan must have been reasonably pleased with the reviews, which praised his ability to evoke moving scenes of city life and country life in a transitional Trinidad of the 1940s and 1950s. For Keith Jardim, *A Day in the Country* is "much more than a generous slice of life", and there is a "deep love of the land in these stories." He singles out "Shadows Move in the Britannia Bar" and "A Day in the Country" for special praise: the former is "wonderfully written", and the latter, he confesses, "has a home in my heart," as it reminds him, in its celebration of life, of Thomas Wolfe's "Circus at Dawn".[2] Chris Searle, too, finds that the stories are "brilliantly realised, without nostalgia, but still with a sense of elegiac truth." For him, "The Red Ball" is especially appealing, for in Khan's description of Bolan's bowling there is the power and grace of Michael Holding and Curtley Ambrose.[3] The writer of the back-cover blurb of *A Day in the Country*, perhaps Poynting himself, describes the collection as "writing to savour beyond place and time". As positive and sympathetic as these reviews are, however, they do not go beyond generalized comments: there is no attempt to analyse Khan's craftsmanship and to investigate the range of the author's thematic concerns in these short stories.

The nine titles, "The Red Ball", "Pooran, Pooran", "The Magic Ring", "Perpetual Motion", "A Day in the Country", "Uncle Rajo's Shoes", "Shadows Move in the Britannia Bar", "Uncle Zoltan" and "Shaving", in themselves, do not indicate any inter-linkages or continuities. Their very discreteness can easily lead the reader to conclude that the short stories were randomly selected. A close reading, however, proves that these short stories were carefully chosen, and that they comprise a collection unified by setting, characterisation, and theme. Khan chose these nine stories, not necessarily because they are his best, but because they are variations on a common theme: the father/son relationship. Even in the three stories, "Uncle Rajo's Shoes", Uncle Zoltan", and "A Day in the Country", the uncle/nephew relationship is, for all intents and purposes, the father/son relationship that is the nucleus of each narrative. To be sure, there may be other ways of categorising them, but these nine pieces can be most meaningfully divided into two groups: the first five stories, "The Red Ball", "Pooran, Pooran", "The Magic Ring", "Perpetual Motion", and A Day in the Country" are adolescent stories that have as their protagonist a young boy. The remaining four are adult stories in which an adult son/nephew interrogates his relationship with his father/uncle, and to a lesser extent, with his mother/aunt.[4]

In the group of adolescent stories, the protagonist is a schoolboy who, like Bolan in "The Red Ball" and Patrick in "The Magic Ring", attends primary school in the city, or like Pooran in "Pooran, Pooran", and the anonymous son in "Perpetual Motion", attends Queen's Royal College in Port of Spain. Both adolescents are no doubt fictional versions of the young Khan, who like them, attended both primary school and secondary school in the capital city.[5] While the characterisation of the adolescent protagonist remains largely unchanging, there are variations of the father figure. On the one hand, there is the kind, understanding father – Uncle Rajo in "A Day in the Country", Ramdath in "Pooran, Pooran", and the Chinese man in "The Magic Ring"; on the other hand, there is the brutal, frustrated, cruel father in "The Magic Ring" who exercises a frightening control over Patrick's tragic life. Between both extremes are two different father figures: the father in "Perpetual Motion" is neither cruel nor brutal; he is obsessed with his machine of perpetual motion and dies because of it, leaving his family in the lurch at the mercy of an embittered grandfather. In "The Red Ball", however, Bolan's father is a victim of displacement and financial anxiety: he has moved to the city from Tunapuna with the specific aim of making money to pay off loans, and to save enough to return to the country financially comfortable.[6] Work, drink, and long hours away from home have distanced him from his son, who, unknown to him, feels the effects of displacement much more deeply than anyone appreciates. After brutally beating Bolan for stealing from his savings, he, with his wife's intervention and pleading, achieves an appreciable measure of sympathy and understanding, indicated by his lying close to his son during the night.

Because the protagonist in each story is either an adolescent male or an adult male, the perspective is, not surprisingly, masculine, as is the general experience depicted. In "Perpetual Motion", the mother is marginalised; in "Shaving", the mother is belittled; and in "Shadows Move in the Britannia Bar", the mother is totally omitted. The predominant masculine perspective, however, does not prevent Khan from presenting some strong female/mother/wife figures. In "Uncle Rajo's Shoes", Bimla, Baldeo's wife of twenty years, boldly asserts her independence by refusing to cook, demanding more money for rent and food, and by regularly leaving her house for her mother's. She wants to keep Baldeo in line by preventing him from coming to terms with his present condition. Baldeo longs to discover the reason for his routinised life; when he, through the agency of Zampi, the obeah man, finally discovers the reason, he hurls Uncle Rajo's belongings, which he has inherited, into a bonfire. Thinking that he has gone mad, Bimla leaves for her mother's with a parting insult: "Waster! Rum-sucker, waster!" (p. 97). Baldeo wins the battle with Uncle Rajo's inheritance, but Bimla shows that she is every bit her husband's equal. Though the relationship between husband and wife is quite different in "Uncle Zoltan", the mother is the only one who is sympathetic to her brother-in-law's plight, even if she is taken in by this confidence man. In "A Day in the Country", Khan presents a strong mother/aunt/wife, who in no uncertain terms rules the roost. She is up before her husband and the rest of the household, and wakes him up with an insult, "You ain't have no shame or what?" She orders the two boys off to have a bath with the cold rain water from the "copper"[7] in the yard and she orders the boys and her husband to breakfast. With "her cool cutting voice", she silences the screaming customers, and she is the one who decides when the lamps would be trimmed. She tries to curtail Uncle Rajo's love of life, when at the end of the business day, she rebukes his habit of kicking his legs high in the air and skipping over the counter as light as a kite: "You playin' young an' strong, [...] When you sprain your back an' take sick in bed don't say I didn't warn you" (p. 77). However, in "The Magic Ring", where Patrick suffers one blow to the head from his father when he is two years old that makes him cross-eyed, and another when he is ten years old that sets his eyes right but leaves him dumb, the mother is helpless before the father's violence. In "The Red Ball", Khan presents his most compelling portrait of the assertive and influential mother. She is afforded insights into her son's feelings that are denied initially to the father. With father away working on the American Base in Chaguaramas, she keeps a close eye on the movements of her only child, and sees him sitting day after day on the concrete runner of Woodford Square, watching other boys playing cricket. When she discovers that he has stolen the money and has bought a ball, she knows that he has been accepted by the city boys. After trying to prevent the brutal beating by the father, she is able with soft and astute words to change her husband's outlook. She knows her husband, grasps her son's plight, and is able to make her husband understand why Bolan has stolen the money. This is a unique moment in the collection: it indicates the triumph of female caring and psychology over the male need to dominate and control. This is the apotheosis of the quiet, strong wife/mother figure.

Khan's craftsmanship ensures that these nine short stories are not simply domestic narratives: their implications go beyond family matters. Khan uses the father/son relationship as a literary vehicle for his interrogation of such issues as the displacement from the country to the city, the negative effects of a colonial education, the toll that unemployment and frustration take on an individual who feels his hold on life slipping away, the old pastoral debate of the ascendancy of the country over the city, the establishment through folklore of the existence of a world beyond science and reason, the need of the individual to create a private romance and mythology as a means of survival, the need to look backward and inward to comprehend one's present situation, and the condition and role of the artist in society. As this study demonstrates, these concerns are not new to Khan's fiction: these short stories, then, continue the issues Khan broached in *The Jumbie Bird* and explored further in *The Obeah Man* and *The Crucifixion*.

In "The Red Ball", Bolan, fresh from the country, is so utterly displaced in the city that his only pastime is a combination of catching the falling blossoms of the pink and yellow poui,[8] putting fireflies in a white phial and letting his feet dangle in the cool water of the fountain in the centre of Woodford Square, where he watches the city boys play cricket.[9] His sitting down day after day on the concrete runner around the outside of the Square symbolizes his displacement and exclusion from city life. The Square, with its flowing fountain water, its flowering trees, its boys at play, its offer of a rustic pastime, is transformed in Bolan's displaced imagination into a citified Tunapuna, whose internalised sights and sounds continually call to him. Small wonder he is drawn to this oasis in the centre of the bustling city. Without considering the young boy's feelings, months before, his father "left their ajoupa hut in Tunapuna [...] loaned out his two cows to his uncle", borrowed money, and moved to the city to work as a "cutlassman" on the American base in Chaguaramas. The move from country to city means opportunities for both father and son: the father can earn much more money than he can make in Tunapuna, and the son can enjoy the benefits of a city education. The dutiful wife goes along with her husband's vision, thinking of him and her only child. The father becomes so wrapped up in his menial work that he begins to spend longer hours away from home. Nothing in the narrative suggests that while becoming more preoccupied with working and earning more money, he considers what is happening to Bolan. Indeed, he indirectly blames Bolan for the family's inability to forge ahead financially: "Is always the same damn thing. Soon as you have a shilling save... two shillings expense come up. As soon as we did have a li'l money save we have to go and get a ... [child]" (p. 13). Not only does he embarrass the boy who, because of the confines the barrack room, is forced to listen to the conversation between mother and father, but also he fails to respect his son as an individual. Such is the neglect of his only son that the mother upbraids him for forgetting Bolan's name, and in so doing, denying him his identity: "What come over you at all? The child have a name, and it look as if you even forget that too" (p. 14).

Bolan's father even forgets to consider what life in the strange city might be doing to his son, and broadly labels the boy's time away

from home as "idl[ing] away his time." At school, things are no better
as he is given "six lashes in the palm" for daydreaming when the
crowing of a rooster takes his mind back to the "smells and sounds"
of Tunapuna. Both father and teacher, then, work in concert to
destroy his identity, his individuality, his growing sense of belonging
and self-worth. Where many, perhaps most boys would have capitu-
lated, Bolan does not. Khan endows the boy with a vision and courage
to do what he has to do to establish his individuality and sense of
being accommodated in the new, unfriendly environment. After
being sent to sleep, he overhears a conversation between his parents
in which they reveal how much money they have saved since moving
to the city, and where the money is kept. He instinctively knows the
risk he has to take to rescue his waning self-esteem: he steals the
money and buys a brand-new red cork ball, a symbol of his initiative
and initial success in the city. This brings him a satisfaction and pride
offered no where else in the city; it establishes his credentials as the
star bowler of the team, as he is soon lionised by his teammates.
Buoyed by his success with the ball and the acceptance by his peers,
he sees another opportunity to consolidate his acceptance. He treats
his teammates to their fill of black pudding.[10] Bolan's elation is short-
lived as his irate father calls him away from his friends and once in the
yard administers a cruel beating, seeing his son as a product of his
wife's side of the family and as a traitor to him and his side. Blinded
by anger, self-righteousness, and an obsession to establish his authority, he shows no mercy, only stopping when he is too tired to
continue the beating. Mother takes away the switch, rescues and
comforts her son, and takes control. Fortunately, for this family,
whether father acknowledges it or not, mother in her quiet, measured way is in charge. For unknown to both father and son, she "had
gone down several days looking for the boy and seen him on the
runner watching the other boys play…" She never forgot her son's
proficiency with the ball in the country, nor did she fail to grasp the
significance of his sitting on the runner. When she takes out the ball
from his pocket after the beating, she realizes not only that "they had
finally asked him to play," but also that he had taken his first big step
in being acculturated to city life. She recognises what the red ball
means to her son: a symbol of his desire to belong and to succeed in
this new life which has been thrust upon him.

Her pride in her son's initiative and success mingles with her sympathy, and as Bolan tries to sleep, she, in whispers, opens her husband's eyes to the reality of what has happened. As he sees only the negative aspects of Bolan's act, she no doubt emphasises the positive. Though whispering, she is forceful, articulate, and convincing. As father edges close to lie beside his son, we sense that the mother's quiet intercession has afforded him a timely insight into his son's life of adjustment and belonging. Bolan's dream of the great man standing in the bowl of the fountain in Woodford Square speaking to him is Khan's way of making his fiction realistic. For the link between the father and the great man, and between the "smiling women seated back to back to back at the feet of the standing man" and the mother is established as early as the fourth paragraph of the narrative. Two acts, it appears, occur simultaneously: Bolan's dream that the great man had said, "We love you like nothin' else in this whole world... must always remember that" (p. 17), and his father's lying close to him. Though his father's pride would not allow him to confess his love for his son, Bolan no doubt grasps the significance of his parents' conversation, of his dream, of the lingering smell of his father's body, and of his waking in the morning. Because of his mother, this is the dawn of a new day in the life of this family: there is no longer any need to steal, nor any need for beatings, as father and son are reconciled to each other.

Like "The Red Ball", "The Magic Ring" is set in a Port of Spain yard, almost certainly the very yard in which Manko in *The Crucifixion* takes up residence and the yard Khan frequented as a young boy. Like "The Red Ball", "The Magic Ring" is a story of violence, abuse, and the effects of the consumption of alcohol, though it takes them further. "The Red Ball" is a tragicomic narrative, in which there is at the end a reconciliation between father and son; however, "The Magic Ring" is unrelieved tragedy. Patrick's father is a victim of a double displacement: he has been displaced from the country, and he has been displaced from his occupation. Life in the city has flattered to deceive: "...at one time he had two men in his employ and he thought himself a rich man" (p. 37). Fourteen years in the city and loss of employment have taken their tragic toll on Patrick's father. They have reduced him to a cruel, violent father, an abusive misogynist, a racist – easily the most despicable adult male character in all of Khan's fiction, reminiscent of, but worse than, Santo Pi, Massahood's cruel grandfather in *The Obeah Man*. Fourteen years of marriage have created a husband who resents his wife and a father who resents his only child, Patrick, born on St Patrick's day, but ironically denied the luck of the Irish. Indeed, it is hard to imagine an adolescent, or anyone, more unfortunate than Patrick. To the husband, his wife, like all women, is "too stupid in the world today", and "without any sense in [her] head" (p. 35). His son is too much his mother's son for him to have any respect for the ten-year-old boy. He looks at and listens to both with "disdain", "disgust", "scorn", and "hate." His egotism and misogyny do not permit him to see or even to acknowledge another point of view.

In spite of his wife's constant defiance, he has managed to maintain rigid control over her and their son. She is bitter, frustrated, and exasperated. She has had to live with the awful reality that her normal child was rendered cross-eyed when he was two years old by a violent slap from the father. Not surprisingly, the father has absolved himself from any blame, convincing himself that the boy's condition is her fault, and suggesting strongly that she has been unfaithful: "Everybody know that when a child born with a ko-kee-eye, that it is because he moomah do something wrong when she was carrying he in she belly" (p. 39). Indeed, he blames his wife not only for his son's condition but also for his own present condition. Life, he remonstrates, is unfairly feminine, "No matter how hard a man work in this world, he never get thanks for it." He has made life for his wife and son a hellish nightmare. Fortunately, she has the equanimity and patience to withstand his taunting and provocation, and the self-possession and wisdom not to make a bad situation worse: "She had a small kitchen knife in her hand, and she hurled it out into the yard out of fear and compulsion; she was afraid that she would be compelled to do some violence with it" (p. 38)

Like his mother, Patrick lives in fear of his father's abuse and violence. Consequently, at the age of ten, he has become a solitary wanderer through the city streets, discovering places of interest and making a few adult friends along the way. Unlike Bolan, he is city-born and city-bred, without any memories of a comforting past in the country. In his daily wanderings he has discovered alternative father figures, who are kind and sympathetic: the pharmacist, the jeweller, and especially the Chinese coal-shop owner, who makes it possible for him to own the magic ring, which changes his life. Patrick is a tragic victim of a wicked, violent father, who wilfully, by his blows, crosses and uncrosses his eyes, leaving him at the end with normal sight, but voiceless, and by implication, without an identity. Nothing in the narrative even hints at a possibility of change in the father's outlook or behaviour. We are left to imagine him incapacitating Patrick further, or even killing him with another blow to the head. Tragically, Patrick's mother does not have the leverage to negotiate with the father to elicit sympathy and understanding. Things turn around for Bolan because of the mother's advocacy; things, however, become worse for Patrick because of the father's overbearing egocentrism.

Unlike "The Red Ball" and "The Magic Ring", "Pooran, Pooran" has a sustained double focus: the two equipollent topoi are the home and the school. Pooran's adolescent life oscillates between what the parents, with best intentions, choose for him and what the King George College (without doubt a fictional name for Queen's Royal College) offers him. Pooran who lives in Tunapuna, the village of Bolan's family, too, and who comes from a poor Hindu family, must feel privileged to attend the city college that both Ismith Khan and Jamini in *The Jumbie Bird* attended and that produced such international figures as C.L.R. James, Eric Williams, historian and first Prime Minister of Trinidad and Tobago, and V.S. Naipaul, among others. Though few past students speak ill or negatively about the education they received at Queen's Royal College, there were no doubt students who were not pleased, and others who were disillusioned with their college experience. Most of these, like Pooran, would have come from the country, only to face discrimination and racial and class prejudice. Its name, the predominance of foreign white masters during Khan's schooling there, its uniform complete with tie, are unmistakable indices of the colonial nature of this illustrious college. C.L.R. James in the autobiographical *Beyond A Boundary* gives this crucial assessment: "As schools go, it was a very good school, though it would have been more suitable to Portsmouth than to Port of Spain" (p. 37).

At the end of *The Jumbie Bird*, Jamini, who has been given the chance of a lifetime to attend Queen's Royal College, through the bold initiative of his forward-looking grandmother, complains to his father, Rahim, that he feels out of place at the institution: "It's not the school so much, it's the boys. I just feel as if I don't belong there... I feel as if I'm in gaol every day. I don't like the way the yard smells,

I don't like the way the classrooms smell…" (p. 221). Khan, himself, confessed to feeling out of place in Queen's Royal College among the majority of privileged middle-class boys. In "The Red Ball", Bolan is victimised at his primary school, and beaten for his daydreaming. The criticism of education that is implicit in these two works becomes full-blown in "Pooran, Pooran", where Khan unleashes a scathing critique of the education that Pooran receives, and by extension of colonial education in general.

There are different levels of tragic experience in "Pooran, Pooran". As in "The Red Ball" and "The Magic Ring", the mother is the one who through dedication and commitment keeps house and home together. Like Bolan's mother, Pooran's is a woman of vision, endorsing the value of a formal education. She convinces her husband, who had suggested that Pooran "… go down to Sadhu… learn Bhagavad-Gita, Ramayan… and learn about life" (p. 19) that the boy should instead go to the "city college". Ramdath is a traditionalist in suggesting that his son learn what he and generations before him imbibed through the oral tradition from pundits. Yet he does not want his son to "spend his life in the sugarcane fields". He therefore acquiesces in Leela's decision because he realises that it is the solution to his and Pooran's dilemma. Indeed, historically, formal non-Hindu, non-Muslim education, in other words, colonial education, proved the solution to the Indo-Trinidadian problem of social mobility. Leela and Ramdath, of course, are acting in the best long-term interests of their only child; but without any personal experience of formal education, they are at a loss as to what it is all about. Their only tenuous connection with it is through their perfunctory conversations with the fledging college student.

Khan makes Pooran atypical of his generation in his rejection of the promise of formal education and in his plea to his father, "Babooji, can I go with you to plant the sugarcane fields?". But Khan makes it clear that what Pooran rejects is not formal education; rather it is the kind and quality of education offered at the city college. At first, Pooran is insulted and humiliated by racists Sharpe and Glenford as they desecrate his lunch so lovingly prepared by Leela; roti and bhaji, staple food for generations of Indo-Trinidadians, rich and poor, is reduced to "cardboard and grass" by the two white boys, one of whom, no doubt with disgust and scorn, "took a pencil and poked in and out of the spinach leaves, piercing tiny holes into the roti with his pencil point" (p. 27). Pooran is encouraged to believe that he can have a meaningful "camaraderie with Mr Hopkins," referred to by the boys as "the mad man in the Science Block". The young boy's expectation of education at the college is once more buoyed up, and he no doubt feels a sense of satisfaction in Mr Hopkins's censure and punishment of Glenford for not preparing the morning lesson. His belief in Mr Hopkins grows daily, and for the moment school life is exciting. Tragically, it is this teacher in whom he places most faith who destroys the young boy's belief in education. For Mr Hopkins's view of education is as mistaken as it is reductive. He reduces the overwhelming complexity of life to a "speck of jelly" on "a glass slide," and is decidedly more fascinated by death than by life. Instead of bringing the injured, starving pup back to good health, as Pooran excitedly hopes he will, Mr Hopkins instructs the duped boy how to snuff out its tenuous life: "We'll pickle it tomorrow" (p. 30). He further reduces all education to science, never finding time to encourage his students to respond to the beauty and mystery of living nor to religion or spiritual truth. It is Hopkins's reductive, lopsided teaching that turns Pooran off and away from formal education. His pedagogy, aimed at improving the mind, is soul-destroying. His teaching and that of Pooran's parents collide and present for the young boy a mind-wrenching dilemma. Pooran is eager to absorb the information of formal education, yet he cannot reconcile Hopkins's science with traditional Hindu teaching. Hopkins has reified crea- tion; Hinduism fills it with wonderful aromas, tastes, beauty, mys- tery, and life, orchestrated by the little gods and the big gods.

The "horror" on Leela's face is surely a combination of the knowledge that she has been mistaken in not heeding the advice of Ramdath and Sadhu and the recognition of what Pooran is rejecting. Given her forward-looking vision, she believed she was acting in the best interests of both Pooran and the family. She allows her faith in what she perceives as being progressive to override her instinctive belief in the value of the teaching of Hinduism. When a sympathetic and indulgent Ramdath acquiesces in Pooran's articulate pleading, Leela knows that her son has missed the chance for social mobility. Not having embraced the opportunity, he must spend his life in the canefields. For Pooran, too young to appreciate what lies ahead, life in the canefields is preferable to living in a world according to Hopkins. Given the intellectual gap between what Pooran learns and what the parents know, the young boy has no one to turn to and believes that he has made the right decision. He believes that he has declared his allegiance to working with his father in the canefields rather than to learning from Hopkins at the city college, to life rather than to death, to the future rather than to the present. What Pooran cannot at this juncture grasp is the reason why his parents have sent him to the city college. Hopkins's teaching drives him to reject his best chance for intellectual maturation and the attendant social mobility.

Unlike "Pooran, Pooran", "Perpetual Motion" and "Uncle Zoltan" both focus on the artist figure. In "Perpetual Motion", the father, having created several smaller inventions, is working on his magnum opus, a machine of perpetual motion which will make men free. Predictably, most of his waking moments are spent on the machine, and he seldom finds time to eat or interact meaningfully with his family. So obsessed is he with his machine and its guiding principle that he mentally and emotionally carries them wherever he goes: into the Britannia Bar and into Woodford Square; the former a place of refuge and comfort; the latter with its racist rabble-rousers, a potentially dangerous place. It is here, in this Square, which embraces and offers the young Bolan a chance to establish himself and to belong, that the father is fatally stabbed. It is ironic that the politicians whom he "particularly disliked" because of their empty promises to make men free, are the ones who create the fatal situation. When the Black Power speaker rhetorically asks the identity of "the enemy", the father, obsessed with his ongoing masterpiece, blurts out, "Friction… you fool… friction is the enemy" (p. 64). Khan focuses on the huge divide between politician and the artist, between the man of empty words and the man whose imaginative creations point the way forward. Politics snuffs out the life of the artist, the man of vision, the individual, daring enough to offer a new definition of freedom. In this, the most autobiographical of the short stories, Khan endorses the struggle of his father's dedication to invention: "I cannot hold with those who take the view that our happiness comes when we surrender… When we give up all the notions of happiness we once had. That resembles resignation, and Papa was never resigned" (p. 59). Khan also endorses the artist's necessary commitment to the "idea" (reminiscent of Marlow in *Heart of Darkness*) and to the execution of it.[11] Though the mother is understandably angry with her husband and his death, her inability to enter the world of the artist is seen as a failure. Khan conflates his adolescent protagonist's sympathy for his father's commitment with his own understanding of the condition of the artist in a society that is insensitive to his true role therein. "Perpetual Motion" demonstrates the tragedy that results from the misunderstanding between the politicians and the purblind society they lead, on the one hand, and the artist who resists being led, on the other.

In "Uncle Zoltan", Khan presents an artist of a different kind: Uncle Zoltan is among a long line of confidence men in literature. Compared to others, he seems harmless, more to be humoured than feared. He has read H. Rider Haggard's *She*, his favourite book, and after many readings deduces the author's intentions. Grasping the difference between reality and romance, he attempts to emulate the nineteenth-century author. He sets about creating his own romantic narrative about his killing of a man and his having to "lay low" in the bush. Taken to court for child support, and fined by the magistrate, and subsequently jailed, he, the black sheep of the family, seizes the opportunity of creating a private mythology, as it were. The narrative establishes that Uncle Zoltan is not a victim of a desperate wife nor of harsh laws; he knows what he is doing, and, like the experienced actor, studies his every move. His calculated brazenness to his father-in-law to avoid court costs has the desired effect: "The old man all but fainted. His body became rigid; he could not even move a limb to strike Uncle Zoltan, so great was his rage" (p. 119). Also, he understands the value of playing the gentleman in jail to win the respect and favour of the turnkeys. Somewhat like Alan Quartermain, Haggard's questing hero, Uncle Zoltan finds ordinary life less attractive and compelling than the lure of romance. When everyone else in the family avoids him, he is able to charm and convince his sister-in-law, who is something of an artist herself, to help him. She and her son, the anonymous narrator, both find Uncle Zoltan intriguing: she believes his story of murder and gives him the five dollars he asks for; the son, when he returns from America, goes in search of elusive Uncle Zoltan and also allows himself to be duped. For the narrator, Uncle Zolton is an intriguing figure of romance, "who leads one of the most isolated and curious kind of lives" (p. 128). When he gives Uncle Zoltan five dollars, after hearing the identical story told to his mother, he knows his quest is over. The narrator has been ushered into a world of everyday romance by a self-styled mythopoeist, whose measured gestures and dark tale of murder and hiding will continue to haunt his nephew's imagination, though far removed from the land of his birth.

In "Uncle Rajo's Shoes", Baldeo, like Uncle Zoltan, is searching for a solution to his humdrum existence. In Bimla and Baldeo, husband and wife, Khan presents two essentially different individuals: Bimla, without question, accepts her lot in life; Baldeo finds no comfort in answers he has inherited, and continually questions his opinions and behaviour. His questions may strike some readers as banal, as do Foster's in Selvon's *An Island Is A World*, but they relate to his constricted experience and suggest his real difficulty in coming to terms with the human condition. The inheriting of Bimla's uncle's shoes is a literary device for establishing the dangers of accepting life at face value, of simply acquiescing in passed-down values and practices. Baldeo, like the much younger Bolan, needs to find himself, to establish his individuality and identity. He cannot accept the repetitive, monolithic answers of a wife, who has grown tired of her husband. It is not because he is a rum-sucker, as Bimla aggressively insists, but that instinctively he knows, as Khan must have known, that he can find answers in the Britannia Bar. For Khan in this short story, and throughout his fiction, depicts this particular bar as a microcosm of society; here are to be found Carnival masqueraders, professionals, obeah men, ordinary men and women, the lonely and frustrated. Khan insists in his fiction that going to the bar is not running away; on the contrary, it is where one confronts life and finds solutions to problems. With the help of Zampi, the obeah man, who we must assume is the same individual as the protagonist of Khan's second novel, Baldeo eventually discovers the answer to his gnawing question. Zampi, who has with difficulty discovered his own answers, leads him to look inward, to discard the answers of others, to establish an individual identity: "He had found out in his own stumbling way [...] You found answers by yourself; they were within you all along, somewhat hidden, but you could find them. There was nothing wrong with him. What was wrong was the world that surrounded him, a world filled with answers, all the wrong answers" (p. 100) As the bonfire reduces Uncle Rajo's belongings to ashes, Baldeo experiences a massive release, an emotional rebirth, and a wholeness: "where it had seemed in the past that his mind and body were two different people pulling in different directions, they now seemed like one […]" (p. 101). (This, we recall, is the ideal vision espoused both Zampi in *The Obeah Man* and by Khan himself). As with Tiger in *A Brighter Sun*, the persistent questions are eventually replaced with a final statement of resolve and confidence: "tomorrow I shall go to Bimla's parents and bring her home" (p. 102).

If "Uncle Rajo's Shoes" establishes the need to find personal and individual answers, then "Shadows Move In the Britannia Bar" establishes the need to believe in a world beyond reason and science. To Mr Hopkins, folklore no doubt would be pure nonsense, but to Khan and to Sookoo, it is an interrogation of an experiential dimension beyond the ordinary and the mundane. Sookoo has a firsthand experience with La Diablesse, the *femme fatale* of island folklore, and lives to tell of his adventure. But as spellbinding as that account is, it is not as meaningful as his personal story of his relationship with his ungrateful son. The point of the story is not that ingratitude in a child is sharper than a serpent's tooth, but that obeah is real and powerful. Sookoo's attempts to undo his son's obeah fail because he lacks the necessary faith: "…it look like he ent believe in the obeah man at first, so the obeah man can't do much for him" (p. 113) Acquiring the requisite faith is a lived experience as he utters in his deathbed confession: "Oh God, boy… you come at last? You come at last? Been waiting for you so long" (p. 115). Sookoo is Khan's Ancient Mariner, spiritually oppressed by an awful truth for which recounting the agony is the only solution. Like the old man of the sea, Sookoo knows where to go and to whom to tell his tale. Though we are not afforded insight into the response of the sceptical listeners, we sense that they, like the Wedding Guest, are left wondering, pondering, and tottering on the brink of two worlds.

A quite different short story is the titular "A Day in the Country", at the heart of which is the traditional conflict of pastoral literature. Ten-year-old Chan, who has been reared in the city, spends the August vacation with his twelve-year-old cousin, Kemal, who lives in Tunapuna, which up to the early nineteen-sixties would have generally been considered country. City-bred Chan is glad to leave the "city of Port of Spain, with its confusing streets, automobiles, bicycles, tramcars, and people constantly on the move" (p. 73), to enjoy rustic life with its "peculiar leisureliness", where the life of the senses can be indulged and enjoyed to the full. Country-bred Kemal, however, has grown tired of the country, which, according to him, offers no opportunity for personal growth. Not able, as Chan does, to drink from the nourishing springs of country life, Kemal, like colonial man, begins to look outward for answers. Encouraged by the movie he and Chan cycle to watch, he makes his decision: "'I want to go up there [America] one day and do something like that. No more island for me. Soon, soon, soon, as I grow up I leavin'… leavin' for good'" (p. 83). At this tender age, he decides to turn his back on his island home, reduced in his outward-looking mind to a place of "mosquito, […] dark, [and] pitch oil lamp" (p. 83). First, he gets Chan to agree to exchange places, because, as he sees it, his younger cousin is "lucky to be living in Port of Spain not here in the bush." "The bush" is Khan's and the Trinidadian's phrase for describing all that is remote, stifling, and backward in island culture.

A more sensitive Chan, however, cannot imagine a happier life. But his sensitivity goes well beyond the sights, aromas, and sounds of the country, as indicated by his musing of "the man with the shining cutlass", who, according to the policeman, showed no respect for the king. Chan listens to the accused man's defiant words, and as the two boys race away from the thickening crowd, he feels as though he "had betrayed the man who stood alone with his cutlass" (p. 82). Chan's feeling of betrayal not only evinces an uncommon sympathy at such a tender age, but also suggests an incipient questioning of the rules foisted on colonial man. This is all the more remarkable because Chan has been reared in the city, where laws are more strictly enforced than in the country. In addition, Chan's love of and sensitivity to the country is especially admirable at a time in the economic evolution of the island, when oil was gradually supplanting agriculture, creating on the face of adults a "strange confusion". Khan, somewhat like Chan, betrays his own preferences in his choice of imagery: "They had worked on their small plots of land, planting sugarcane or vegetables, selling their produce by the wayside, and then suddenly they were working the bizarre machinery that stood like lordly giants on the fenced-off refinery, lit up by night to show off some arrogant splendour in the bright silver-painted tubes coiling around and about" (p. 76). Reminiscent of the mechanical harvester in Selvon's *The Plains of Caroni*, the oil refinery is Khan's version of the machine in the garden, "bizarre machinery" that has begun its destruction of an accustomed way of life, largely that of Indo-Trinidadians.

The final story of the collection is unique in the narrator's choice of language and in the choice of its central literary symbol. The narrator's language oscillates between island vernacular and standard English, no doubt practised when he was sent "all the way up to America to study at a university". The anonymous narrator closely resembles that of "Uncle Zoltan", but this one is more introspective and analytical; this is a much more serious, nostalgic narrative. From the outset, Khan establishes shaving as a masculine activity that allows the individual who possesses an artistic sensibility the privilege of introspection. For neither shaving nor introspection is possible without a mirror. The Trinidad-born narrator, far removed geographically from the "land of [his] birth," sits in a "draughty Brooklyn basement" and feels the need to shave. An electricity outage makes his electric razor useless. He rummages in his suitcase and finds an old safety razor, a legacy of his mother's pragmatism, and stands before a "large", "ornate," and "antique" mirror. For the narrator and Khan, this is the combination of all the other mirrors in the story: Sookoo's small oval, the great oval of the "big-bureau-mirror", and the "crack-up" rectangle, held together by the ends of postage stamps. In this "relic," the narrator sees all the faces and personalities that have "shaved" and fashioned him – mother, father, and Sookoo, the itinerant barber who gave him his first shave. It is the look of this first shave that elicits a linguistic response that haunts the narrator's imagination. It becomes for him the link that conflates the defining moments of his life. Introspection here is necessarily retrospection: the narrator's life is reflected and refracted prismatically through the four mirrors. The narrative itself becomes the ultimate and most capacious mirror, affording the audience not only a reflection of faces, shaved and unshaved, but also telling insights into their minds, feelings, and relationships. As these faces disappear from the antique mirror, "as in a dream", the kaleidoscopic narrative dimensionalises the four major players into a compelling freeze-frame, creating Khan's most innovative and introspective short story.

Notes

1. Information provided by Ismith Khan in an unpublished conversation with Roydon Salick (August 2001).
2. *Trinidad Guardian,* 4 August 1998.
3. <www. peepaltreepress.com/review display asp? rev id=87>
4. One other way of categorising these stories is to see five as Indo-Trinidadian stories. In "Perpetual Motion", "The Magic Ring", "Shaving", and "Uncle Zoltan" there is little or nothing to determine the ethnicity of the protagonists and others, although there is natural assumption, because of the author's ethnicity, that they are, too, Indo-Trinidadian stories. "Pooran, Pooran", incidentally, is the only short story in which ethnicity is a central issue.
5. Khan's schooling in the city is outlined in my "Introduction".
6. Tunapuna, featured in three of these stories, is approximately eight miles east of Port of Spain and two miles from St Joseph, the island's first capital. As a boy, Khan spent many happy vacations in Tunapuna at his maternal uncle's home. Tunapuna, incidentally, is the birthplace of C.L.R James, perhaps the finest intellect this region has produced.
7. A "copper" is a large iron (formerly copper) basin "varying in size from 4 to 6 ft in diameter and up to $2^{1}/_{2}$ ft deep", in which cane-syrup was boiled in the factories (Allsopp, p. 168). When discarded, it was used as a drinking receptacle for animals (especially horses and water buffalo) on the sugar estate and as a receptacle for gathering rain water on private properties. Though widely considered a Caribbeanism, the *OED* establishes that "copper" entered the language as early as 1667 as a standard word.
8. Few trees can match in beauty the flowering poui. While there are a few shades of the pink poui (*tabebuia pentaphylla* or *rosea*), it is hard to imagine a deeper, brighter yellow than the blossom of the yellow poui (*tabebuia serratifolia*). Both trees can still be found in Woodford Square, the expansive playground of the young Khan.
9. Although "Bolan" is a fairly common name in Trinidad, Khan intentionally puns on the first syllable of the star bowler's name.

10. "Pudding", when it refers to the ubiquitous blood sausage (made most frequently with pig's blood), is almost always pronounced "pudd'n" in Trinidad. Khan throughout his life was very fond of black pudding, and said more than once that the best pudding he tasted was sold by a woman in St Helena.

11. Khan's father, Faiez, was, according to Khan, the finest jeweller and watch-repairer of his time in Port of Spain. He spent his time away from making jewellery and repairing watches on a machine of perpetual motion. Johnny, the wretched jeweller (a drunk and an arsonist) in *An Island Is a World*, who is also working on a machine of perpetual motion, is Selvon's unflattering, fictional portrait of Faiez Khan (see n. 8, *The Jumbie Bird*).

CONCLUSION

In a panel discussion on Indo-Caribbean literature at York University, Ontario, Khan names two concerns that preoccupy him as a writer, namely, "language and identity". [1] He adds, "When I was growing up in Trinidad I wished I could see or read something in which the protagonist was someone like myself, spoke my language and was in situations like mine." Khan's novels and short stories illustrate his point, for in them he creates protagonists we can identify with and who speak a language we understand, whether it be Trinidad Standard or the vernacular. Following the lead of Selvon and Naipaul, Khan developed a fine ear for the different registers of island English. The opening sections of *The Crucifixion*, discussed earlier (pp. 76-78), are wonderful examples of Khan's ability to reproduce authentically the sound, rhythm, and intonations of Trinidad English. We hear the dispassionate Standard of the outsider voice commenting on what he sees looking in, and we are carried along by the lilt of the vernacular of the insider voice, convincing us that he is one of the yard folk with pivotal questions to ask and tales to tell. The language used, therefore, is quite often a (perhaps *the*) defining quality of the speaker as he attempts to establish his identity. Kale Khan's commanding tone and language tells us so much about this self-styled leader of men, as does the quiet, defiant language of Binti, whose sacrifice in the face of tremendous odds gives the family a new start and fresh hope; Hop and Drop's acerbity is a mirror of his tortured mind and twisted identity; Zampi's measured language is a reflection of his struggle to attain a definitive equilibrium; and Manko's violent condemnation of wrongdoing is a function of his tragic over-zealousness. Khan employs a variety of stylistic strategies to bring his characters to life.

One strength of Khan's style, not commented on by the majority of critics, is its poetical quality. Even the unsympathetic critic is hard-pressed not to agree with Blundell: "He [Khan] is a novelist who writes with the economy and perception of a poet".[2] There are so many memorable passages that we can choose at random. Where Naipaul is content with a strong, unequivocal sentence, Khan is often acutely lyrical. The entire "Prologue" to *The Jumbie Bird* is arguably pure poetry, vibrating with its peculiar rhythm and imagery; it does what poetry does best: it takes an ordinary object and transforms it into a poetic symbol. A pygmy owl is invested with a mythology of mortality, making it not simply a bird of ill omen, but a godlike creature with a special relationship with man. The opening of Chapter Four of *The Obeah Man* is special because of its poetry; it emphasises the tyranny of the sun and the painful protraction of time in the tropics. So is the beginning of the thirteenth chapter of *The Jumbie Bird*, which also describes the power of the sun, and where Khan's assessment of island life is summed up in a simple, provocative statement: "In no place but the tropics are life and death so close" (p. 163). The opening of Chapter Six of *The Obeah Man*, more than any other passage in Khan's fiction, provides compelling evidence of the power of his poetic prose:

> The pool of Blue Basin is a low bowl hammered out deep into the ground by the pounding waters. Its blue water rarely sees the daylight. In the afternoon the basin grumbles in near darkness, the earth around it cool and damp, and a fine spray of the hammering waters scrubs the thick wide leaves a glistening green, covering them until the tiny droplets, hugging one another, caressing one another, rush to finally become one. They stand still for a moment in this ecstasy, roll into the fork of a leaf, then into the earth where they are absorbed thus locked together. By evening, at the first dewfall, the ground is pungent with an aroma of the great wide, waxy leaves that hide the face of the earth from the thirsty mouth of the sun. It is a strange odour that rises from the basin… one that is so close to life, yet not living. When the obeah man first came here he thought, as children do, that this odour was 'life', that all the shades of meaning of the word 'life' were contained in this smell of the basin, and in such moments he was happy, pleased with all the world about him, for the earth in this spot seemed as if awaiting a single breath into its nostrils for life to begin in all its shapes and forms in an otherwise uninhabited planet… (p. 43)

Khan may very well have had Coleridge's unforgettable description of Kubla's "pleasure dome" in mind as he paints his version of Blue Basin, pristine, deep and unspoilt, when he was growing up. Where Coleridge's impetus comes from *Purchas's Pilgrimage* and a dose of laudanum, Khan's derives from the marriage of his mind and one of his favourite haunts, to which he regularly cycled in his youth. In true Wordsworthian fashion, Khan's poetic imagination, as it were, removes the film of custom, and sees into the very life of the natural object, transforming it in the process into something a hundred times more beautiful. As Khan's imagination draws on its remembered familiarity with this "spot", it cannot but choose a particular pattern of images. The imagery moves from the external violence of "hammering" and "pounding", to the restraint of violent feelings in "grumbles", to "scrubs," which nicely negotiates between a natural, earthy violence and the erotic and coital. This is a natural equivalent of the sexual roughness desired and experienced by Zampi and Zolda: "He threw one arm round her bosom, gripping her breast with a kind of savage love… She hammered upon his shoulders with slow deliberate blows… And as his body worked, he felt the rhythm of hers growing closer to the phase of his movements, and then he heard her say: 'Bite me, Zampi … bite my breasts'"(pp. 50-51). This synchronicity between nature and the lovers augurs well for a fulfilling relationship in this sequestered paradise. The "first dewfall", "strange odour", "life, yet not living", and "as if waiting a single breath into its nostrils for life to begin", with its biblical echoes, suggest something creational about Zampi's initial experience with Blue Basin, making him a sort of New World Adam. Fittingly, he responds with childlike wonder and misapprehension to this glorious landscape. Realising like the God of Genesis that it is not good for man to be alone ("otherwise uninhabited"), Zampi goes to find his Eve. He is not put to sleep to lose a rib; rather, he rouses himself from troubled slumber ("He awoke with a sense of strangeness"(p. 19)) – awakening is a recurrent image and motif in Khan's fiction – and he goes in search of her, overcomes many obstacles, and brings her to this edenic spot to live according to the dictates of nature.

Khan's mastery of pacing, of mixing rhythms and cadences, necessary to create variety, tension, and credibility, is best exemplified in the final chapter of *The Jumbie Bird*, as brilliant a piece of writing as any in West Indian literature. Almost in defiance of the "tropic sleep, a crushing sleep" induced by scorching sun, Jamini awakens and finds his Dada's room empty and meticulously tidied. The young boy's mind finds no rest as he has misgivings about the absence of his grandfather. His anxiety is mirrored in his frantic movements:

> It was still early in the afternoon, yet he felt that time was running out as he looked everywhere for Kale Khan. Each time he saw a turban bobbing up and down, he ran ahead to see the face of the man wearing it. People looked at him as he stared them in the face then turned and went away. In the food stalls where people had begun milling he roamed back and forth. [...] His pace slowed and he began to feel that standing in one spot would be as good as running back and forth. But this lasted only a few moments only before he began moving again.
> The sun was going down, and he was tired. He turned into one of the small streets in St James in complete dejection, and there was Lakshmi. (p. 165)

The pace of the narrative comes to a virtual halt, as there is little physical activity, though there is anxiety. The pace then increases slowly, then peters out in their perfunctory consummation amidst the tombs of Lapeyrouse Cemetery:

> They held hands, they walked... they walked... they walked on... They passed an old woman cleaning an overgrown grave ... They walked past groomed graves ... He stopped walking... She sat down in the grass... She was standing... He looked back at her, then turned ... as he walked on. (p. 166)

As he leaves Lakshmi, his quest for his grandfather, temporarily suspended, resumes. The initial feeling that time was running out takes hold of him again. Khan speeds up the pace of his narrative to mirror Jamini's fears:

> The boy shuttled about the crowd... Jamini pushed his way through to see if Kale was among them ... some ran to the corner of a small street where three of the half-moons had come dancing out on the street ... stick players ... cavorted, danced and parried. ... Large bronze cymbals crashed and shot out points of light as they vibrated ... he started back again to the foremost Hussay ... The thousands of onlookers had gone into a bacchanalian frenzy. ... Men who were not stick players ... skipped ... dancing, strutting to the maddening rhythm... (p. 167)

Jamini is too late; perhaps he might have discovered his grandfather in time if he had not stopped to consummate his relationship. But the consummation is necessary as he satisfies a vague longing and desire; and as an era is about to end, he needs to put many things behind him, if he is to move on. Kale's own sense of betrayal by the Commissioner and Hindustan tells him, too, that time is running out. His life, in Macbeth's words, is a "walking shadow", as he moves knowingly to his death, which coincides with the ending of the Hussay ceremony. Khan allows his male protagonist a final ambivalent moment of glory as a stick-fighter, bringing a fitting end to a life of egotism, chagrin, and heroism.

II

A few critics, Ramchand, Poynting, Davies, and Jardim, in addressing particular novels, claim that one weakness in Khan's fiction lies in his inability to create appropriate endings. Poynting argues that the ending of *The Jumbie Bird* is "unnecessarily false" in the sense that Khan seems to feel obliged to create two "deus ex machina devices (the American who brings an order which revives Rahim's jewellery trade and Jamini's grandmother's offer to pay the boy's way through college) to try to make more plausible those commitments [i.e. to the novel's optimistic vision of the future]".[3] This criticism fails to analyse Khan's characterization of Binti from start to finish. From her initial appearance Khan endows his emergent heroine with admirable independence, broad human compassion, a firm business sense, and most of all, an "equilibrium". Though she shares the first quality with Kale, she embodies the others in such a way as to convince us that she will replace him as the head of the family, establishing in the process a progressive heroism that supplants his retrograde, gender-biased heroism. Khan's ambivalent and ironic characterization of Kale makes him a talker; his straightforward presentation of Binti makes her a doer. Kale talks about the need for Jamini to get a good education; Binti makes it possible. Kale's betrayal by the Commissioner is inevitable; but his egotism will not allow him to even consider that possibility. Khan's ending, too, is a reflection of a historical, ethnic reality: in spite of the widespread perception of male dominance, often absolute, in Indo-Trinidadian families, many wives/mothers/grandmothers, in their quiet, measured way, were the true moulders of family life. If we know, too, that Ismith's father's jewellery business at one time flourished partly because of the patronage of tourists, then we are less likely to call the appearance of the American a "deus ex machina" device.

Ramchand, too, has difficulty with the ending of *The Obeah Man*, which for him is "confused" and "too arbitrarily contrived" (p. 127). It is true that Khan does not completely convince us of Zolda's reformation. Yet his realism is established by the ambivalence of the ending. Zolda is Zampi's reward for having overcome all the obstacles that Khan places in his way, not the least of which is his own inner turmoil. Zampi is not given any guarantees, though there is something positive in Zolda's contrition: "But it is my fault... you was right" (p. 142). These are strange words for a woman whose self-absorption has never allowed her to feel or express remorse. Surely, her brush with death brings her to the realisation that life is fragile, and her sensual way, of playing one man against another, has caused two deaths and has almost cost her her life. Those who will not listen must feel; this is a high experiential watershed for Zolda. All this is so new to her; she is jolted into a novel recognition. Khan's lyricism indicates that she comes to recognise that she really loves Zampi, and her former behaviour was posturing:

> Let love live like a lonely lost thing locked up in the heart. It will surface, shine, and see itself again as Zolda saw it now. She would walk along the paths that led up to the waterfall at Blue Basin, she would see all of those things that Zampi had seen without her. She felt there was a gap she wanted to fill in, and she waited to go with him right away with all her sense open so that she would not miss the smallest sound that the winds make when the great sea calls them back from the land. (p. 148)

Both Khan and Zampi give her the benefit of the doubt; the critic ought to do no less. With Hop and Drop and Massahood dead, with her novel remorse and complaisance, the siren call of Carnival will no doubt be less irresistible, as she, far removed from the city, lives out her plea, "'I want to see if I can't find you again and know you like I used to know you'" (p. 144).

Khan's control of his endings is evident, too, in *The Crucifixion*, as he carefully prepares the reader for Manko's final self-deception. From the start, the odds are stacked against this young man, though much admired by his community. Khan pits Manko's well-meaning intention to fulfil his destiny against a system that exists to frustrate and destroy that intention. He is an orphan who lacks significant education. At the orphanage he receives a strait-jacket education; because he is not musically inclined, he is forced to learn a little about the Bible. In a culture where, according to the novel, there are no opportunities for gainful employment for Manko and his kind, the young man has no choice but to become a preacher. Impressed by the older preacher, Manko studies him and carefully emulates him, secure in the knowledge that one day he will be a better and more honest preacher. His preparation is essentially a theatrical perform-ance, which compromises his sincerity. The bustling city calls him, and with emotions almost bursting, he arrives in the city, taking up residence in a yard off Frederick Street. This is a horrible choice, though a necessary one, since his financial situation can afford nothing better. In a real sense, Khan sees the yard not only as a pathetic social reality, but also as a symbol of an inhuman colonial system. Manko tries to rise above the system. Adopting the manner of the colonial masters, he becomes self-righteous and overzealous, all too ready to berate, judge, and condemn his own kind. His self-deception is encouraged first by the yard, then by the yard dwellers. So anxious is Manko to assert his authority and superiority as conductor of the pivotal test, that he may very well have done what Miss Violet initially feared: "What if out of his own spite and his own desire for revenge he let the book fall on purpose?" (p. 99). His importunate need to be crucified recognises that he has "sinned against the Lord"(p. 131), but his tragic lack of self-knowledge does not permit him to grasp that being roped to a cross and pelted with garbage may not make any real difference. The yard, with its poverty, squalor, and ignorance, remains; so does colonialism with its soul-destroying systems. Manko remains a pathetic victim of a vicious system he neither creates nor comprehends.

III

The uniqueness of Khan's fiction has been recognised by the majority of his critics. He has created one-of-a-kind novels, each doing something quite different, and each finding a special niche in West Indian literature. His strengths are many: he is a wonderful story teller who grasps and sustains the reader's interest to the end; he creates such characters as Kale, Binti, Massahood, Zampi, Hop and Drop, Miss Violet, and Manko that stir the imagination long after we put away the books; and he is a thinking novelist who encourages the reader to reconsider his response to historical, political, domestic, and personal issues. Khan's meaningful interiorisation of his two decades of growing up in Port of Spain allows him to create moving scenes of city life. Indeed, Khan is pre-eminently the novelist of Port of Spain: no other Trinidadian writer has written so extensively, cogently, and lovingly of the urban experience. Reading Khan's fiction is grasping the author's prodigious act of memory: far removed in time and geography, he recreates with remarkable clarity and detail the world of childhood and adolescence. In his concern with language and identity he joins his fellow writers in their ongoing attempt to define West Indian man and the society in which he moves and has his being. Lloyd Brown, who has written most intelligently about Khan, deserves the summational word: "Khan's fiction occupies a rather special, though too often neglected niche in Caribbean literature: it celebrates the special vitality of the region's culture without romanticizing it, allowing writer and reader alike to remain painfully aware of the degree to which a sense of social or ethnocultural belonging is often counterbalanced, even thwarted, by persistent isolation and divisiveness between individuals" (*Contemporary Novelists*, p. 497).

Notes

1. "Indo-Caribbean Literature: A Panel Discussion," *Indenture and Exile: The Indo-Caribbean Experience*, Ed. Frank Birbalsingh. (Toronto: TSAR, 1989), p. 142.
2. M.S. Blundell, "*The Obeah Man*," *Caribbean Quarterly* 11 (1965), 95-97.
3. Jeremy Poynting, "Limbo Consciousness: Between India and the Caribbean," *The Toronto South Asian Review* 5:1 (1986), 211.

SELECTED BIBLIOGRAPHY

Primary Sources

Khan, Ismith, *The Jumbie Bird* (London: MacGibbon & Kee, 1961);
    (New York: Obolenksy, 1962); (Toronto: George McCleod,
    1962); (Harlow: Longman, 1985).
— , *The Obeah Man* (London: Hutchinson & Co. Ltd, 1964);
    (Toronto: TSAR, 1995).
— , *The Crucifixion* (Leeds: Peepal Tree Press, 1987).
— , *A Day in the Country and Other Stories* (Leeds: Peepal Tree
    Press, 1994).

Secondary Sources

Allsopp, Richard, *Dictionary of Caribbean Usage* (Oxford: Oxford
    UP, 1996).
Blundell, M.S., "*The Obeah Man*", *Caribbean Quarterly* 11 (1965),
    95-97.
Brown, Lloyd, "The Isolated Self in West Indian Literature",
    Caribbean Quarterly 23 (1977), 54-65.
— , "*The Obeah Man*", *Black Arts Review* 2 (1971), 127-143.
— , "Ismith Khan", *Contemporary Novelists* (New York: St Martins
    Press, 1982), pp. 496-97.
Brown, Stewart, "Introduction", *The Jumbie Bird* (Harlow: Longman,
    1985).
Cobham, Rhonda, "*The Jumbie Bird*: A New Assessment", *Journal
    of Commonwealth Literature* 21:1 (1986), 240-49.
Cummings, James, *Barrack-Yard Dwellers* (Trinidad, St Augustine:
    UWI, School of Continuing Studies, 2004).
Dance, Daryl Cumber, "Conversation with Ismith Khan", *New*

World Adams: Conversations with Contemporary West Indian Writers (Leeds: Peepal Tree Tress, 1992), pp. 121-132.

— , "The Crucifixion", *Journal of West Indian Literature* 2:2 (1988), 48-50.

Davies, Barrie, "The Personal Sense of Society – Minority Views: Aspects of the East Indian Novel in the West Indies", *Studies in the Novel* 4 (1972), 284-295.

Drayton, Arthur, "Ismith Khan", *Fifty Caribbean Writers: A Bio-Bibliographical Critical Sourcebook*, Ed. Daryl Cumber Dance, (Connecticut: Greenwood Press, 1986), pp. 246-54.

— , "Ismith Khan", *Encyclopedia of Post-Colonial Literatures in English*. Ed. Eugene Benson & L.W. Conolly (New York: Routledge, 1994), p. 768.

Foster, Cecil, "Carnival Time", *The Toronto Review of Contemporary Writing Abroad* 13:3 (1995),101-103.

ffrench, Richard, *A Guide to the Birds of Trinidad & Tobago* (Pennsylvania: Harrowood Books, 1980).

Gosine, Ramsamooj, "Caught in a World of Nothing", *Trinidad Guardian,* 19 August 1987.

Greenhaw, Wayne, "A powerful Story of Magic and Myth from Trinidad", Rev. of *The Obeah Man.* <www. forwardreviews.com/ View/ Review.asp? Review ID=18>

"Ismith Khan", *Caribbean Writers-A Bio-Bibliographical-Critical Encyclopedia*, Ed. Donald E. Herdeck (New York: Three Continents Press, 1979), p. 111.

"Indo-Caribbean Literature: A Panel Discussion", *Indenture and Exile: The Indo-Caribbean Experience*, Ed. Frank Birbalsingh, (Toronto: TSAR, 1989), pp. 140-147.

James, C.L.R. "Triumph," *Trinidad* (Xmas 1929).

— , *Minty Alley* (London: Secker & Warburg, 1936; reprint, London: New Beacon Books, 1971).

— , *Beyond A Boundary* (London: Hutchinson & Co, 1963).

James, Louis, *Writers from the Caribbean* (London: Book Trust, 1990).

— , *Caribbean Literature in English* (London: Longman, 1999).

Jardim, Keith, "*A Day in the Country* – A Slice of Life", *Trinidad Guardian*, 4 August 1998.

John, Deborah, "An Old-Fashioned Look at Port of Spain", *Daily Express*, 21 August 1987.

Jones, Margaret, "Between the Pages", *Sunday Guardian*, 24 Nov. 1985.

Juneva, Renu, "Representing History in *The Jumbie Bird*", *World Literature Written in English* 30 (1990), 17-28.

Khan, Ismith, "Dialect in West Indian Literature", *The Black Writer in Africa and the Americas*, Ed. Lloyd Brown (Los Angeles: Hennessey & Ingalls, 1973).

— , "Image and Self-Image in West Indian Writing", *Indians in the Caribbean*, Ed. I. J. Bahadur Singh (New Delhi: Sterling Publishers, 1987).

Katrak, Ketu H., "Ismith Khan", *Dictionary of Literary Biography. Twentieth-Century Caribbean and Black African Writers*, 2nd Series, Ed. Bernth Lindfors & Reinhard Sander (Detroit: Gale Research Inc., 1,1993), pp. 48-53.

Lacovia, R.M., "Ismith Khan and the Theory of Rasa, *Black Images* 1: 3 & 4 (1972), 23-27.

Maes-Jelinek, Hena, "The Novel from 1950 to 1970", *A History of Literature in the Caribbean*, Ed. A. James Arnold (Philadelphia: Benjamin Pub. Co., 2 , 2001), pp. 127-148.

Maes-Jelinek, Hena & Benedicte Ledent, "The Novel since 1970", *A History of Literature in the Caribbean*, Ed. A. James Arnold (Philadelphia: Benjamin Pub. Co., 2, 2001), pp. 149-198.

Nicholson, Betty, "Call of the Cascadura" (2003), 16pp. Unpublished.

Panton, George, "Bacchanal and Cane", *Sunday Gleaner*, 1 Nov. 1964.

Persaud, Sasenarine, "Why Port of Spain comes alive in *The Jumbie Bird*", Interview with Ismith Khan. <www. peepaltreepress . com / review display .asp? rev.id=90>

Poynting, Jeremy, "Limbo Consciousness: Between India and the Caribbean", *The Toronto South Asian Review* 5:1 (1986), 205-221.

Ramchand, Kenneth, "Obeah and the Supernatural in West Indian Literature", *Jamaica Journal* 3:2 (1969), 52-54.

— , "Matters Arising", *Trinidad Guardian*, 11 May, 19 May, 25 May 1988.

"Review of *The Obeah Man*", *Times Literary Supplement*, 15 Oct. 1964, 933.

Salick, Roydon, "Introduction", *The Obeah Man* (Toronto: TSAR, 1995).

Searle, Chris, "Lives in the yard: *The Crucifixion*", Rev. of *The Crucifixion*. <www.peepaltreepress . com / review display asp? rev id=87>

— , "Ismith Khan: *A Day in the Country*", Rev. of *A Day in the Country and Other Stories*. <www. peepaltreepress . com /review display asp? rev. id=86>

Thompson, Ivy, "Review of *The Obeah Man*", *Caribbean Contact* 1:5 18 April, 1973.

Walcott, Derek, "Third Trinidadian Novelist Makes His Bow", *Sunday Guardian*, 22 Oct., 1961.

— , "Critic's Eye View of 1961", *Sunday Guardian* 31 Dec., 1961.

INDEX

ABOUT THE AUTHOR

Roydon Salick, formerly of the Department of Liberal Arts, UWI, St. Augustine, is senior lecturer in the Department of Language, Literature and Caribbean Studies, COSTAATT. He has published articles on Wordsworth and on such West Indian authors as Sam Selvon, Zee Edgell, Michael Anthony, Mervyn Morris, Lionel Hutchinson, Beryl Gilroy and Sonny Ladoo. He has edited *The Poems of Sam Selvon* (2012) and is the author of *The Novels of Samuel Selvon: A Critical Study* (2001) and *Samuel Selvon* (2012).

BY ISMITH KHAN

The Crucifixion
ISBN: 9780948833045; pp. 132; pub. 1987; price: £7.99

When Manko arrives in Port of Spain from his country village to begin his divine mission, he discovers that he has the gift to touch the raw nerve of other people's needs, hopes and guilts. But when he becomes enmeshed in the lives of his fellow yard-dwellers without understanding the different crosses they bear, he sets in train events which teach him too late that there are temptations and responsibilities in being a servant of the Lord for which he is ill equipped. Khan portrays the tensions between authority and freedom, law and love in Trinidadian society through Manko's fate and the stories of the other yard dwellers. Told in two voices, one standard English, the other Creole, *The Crucifixion* is an ironic fable of a tragi-comic self-deception. In exploring the popular folk archetype of the self-crucified preacher, the novel takes the balladic form of the calypso to greater depths.

"A finely constructed and movingly told novel"
– Chris Searle *West Indian Digest*

A Day in the Country & Other Stories
ISBN: 9780948833090; pp. 144; pub. 1994; price: £8.99

In these stories of Indian life in Trinidad in the 1940s and 50s, Ismith Khan brings to vivid life the morning smells of eggplant frying in coconut oil, and herrings baking in the embers of the earthen fireplace; childhoods such as Pooran's, who has to make his way between the poetic mythology of the pundit and the cold, rationalistic materialism of his science teacher, or 'Thiney Boney' who, newly arrived in Port of Spain from the country, has to choose between his new Creole friends and his father's harsh moral certainties. These are not comfortable childhoods, and several stories show the pressures of poverty and despair leading to the abuse of children by their parents. Stories deal with the trauma of urbanisation as Indians are drawn from the country to Port of Spain, though even in the villages, where the shining metal of the oil refineries dwarfs the grasscutter tending his oxen, old ways must change. Ismith Khan brings a tender and affecting style to stories of troubled childhoods, questioning youth and adult struggle.

Keith Jardim writes in *The Trinidad Guardian*: "The brilliant short story 'A Day in the Country' has a home in my heart. It reminded me of the intense, uplifting genius of Thomas Wolfe's short story 'Circus at Dawn'. In both stories the concentration on life, on living, on things seen, heard and felt, is so full and rich that plot becomes unnecessary. But 'A Day in the Country' is much more than a generous slice of life, and it does much more than revel in secure country childhood, or celebrate boyhood in the countryside. It makes a moving, ominous communication about the unsheltering of Trinidad, about its unprepared journey, from the 'Drinking Rum and Coca Cola' years of the 40s and 50s to the bewildering, homogeneous brutality of the 20th century."

OF RELATED INTEREST

Something Rich and Strange: Selected Essays on Samuel Selvon
Ed. Martin Zehnder
ISBN: 9781900715737; pp. 252; pub. 2003; price: £14.99

Critical work on Samuel Selvon has passed through several phases. Initially there was a tendency to treat it as charming, humorous, folksy, naïve and lacking in structure. Then criticism focused on his innovations in the language of narrative and Maureen Warner-Lewis's essay is one of the most brilliant in this framework, demonstrating just how sophisticated and artful was Selvon's play with language register. Another tendency was to treat Selvon's work as expressing a West Indianness that subsumed his own Indo-Caribbean origins. Harold Barrett's essay shows that Selvon's treatment of Indianness always suggests the necessity for it to become part of the Caribbean whole, but without in any sense becoming subsumed. More recent postmodernist treatments of Selvon have seized on the ironic play with intertextuality in his later novels in a way which loses sight of underlying patterns of meaning and social commitment. John Stephen Martin's essay is a salutary restatement of Selvon's humanist philosophy. In short, the essays in this collection both advance the depth of appreciation and understanding of Selvon's fiction and present an admirably balanced range of approaches towards it.

All books available online at www.peepaltreepress.com